CU00926319

To Mike,
With best wishes from
Jeremy Reseigh Watts
Sep. 2009

SCILLY

THROUGH THE EYES
OF THE 'DUCHESS'
OF AURIGA

SCILLY – THROUGH THE EYES OF THE 'DUCHESS' OF AURIGA

SNAPSHOTS OF A BYGONE SCILLONIAN ERA

BY ENA RESEIGH

An affectionate, light-hearted and nostalgic look back
at the Isles of Scilly of the 20th century

written and compiled by

JEREMY RESEIGH WATTS

SHEPHEARD-WALWYN

© Jeremy Reseigh Watts 2005

All rights reserved. No part of this book may be
reproduced in any form without the written permission
of the publisher, Shepheard-Walwyn (Publishers) Ltd

First published in 2005
by Shepheard-Walwyn (Publishers) Ltd
Suite 604, The Chandlery
50 Westminster Bridge Road
London SE1 7QY

British Library Cataloguing in Publication Data
A catalogue record of this book
is available from the British Library

ISBN 0 85683 239 1

Book cover and design by Andrew Candy,
Tentacle Ltd, Greenwich

Printed through Print Solutions,
Wallington, Surrey

TO JOSEPH AND ENA RESEIGH
AND THEIR DAUGHTER JEANNE

A TRIBUTE

AND TO THE PEOPLE OF THE ISLES OF SCILLY,
PAST AND PRESENT – MAY ALL YOUR SCILLONIAN STORIES BE TOLD

While to those who have made the long journey and discovered the secret that is Scilly,
let's keep it just that – a secret!

ACKNOWLEDGEMENTS

I would like to extend my grateful thanks to the following people for their invaluable assistance in the creation of this book:

To my uncle – Peter Joseph Reseigh (Captain Joseph Reseigh's youngest son) for providing historical data and for bringing his personal knowledge to bear.

I would like to express special thanks to Frank Gibson, fourth generation of island photographers in Scilly, for his generosity in allowing me to use his father James Gibson's work in illustrating some of the events during those early years in Scilly – and for putting names and dates to faces and events!

To: Bennie Badcock,
David Badcock,
John Bartlett,
Jean 'Cabin Boy' Blaxall
(for her paintings and cartoons),
Rex Bowley,
Lou and
Sarah-Jayne Boudreau,
Keith Campion
(for patiently answering so many questions!),

journalist Jeremy Clarkson
(for kindly allowing me to plagiarise his poignant Concorde eulogy when lamenting the fate of the Lily of Laguna),
Howard Cooper
of Trinity House,
Daphne Chudleigh,
Peter Ellis,
Wilfred and Dorothy Elvin,

Michael Foster
of 'Jane's Fighting Ships',
Mark Groves,
Michael Hicks,
Alfred Hicks,
the late Joseph Trenear Hicks,
Julie Hicks,
Ron Hicks *(of Bath not Scilly!)*
for the nun joke,
Sue Hicks,

Simon Jarman,
June Lethbridge
and her late husband Richard,
Elizabeth Legg,
Avril and Clive Mumford,
Dr.Martin Parsons BA, PhD
of the University of Reading,
Norah Pender,
John Reseigh
and Joanna Smith.

Special thanks go also to Susan Stockwell LBIPP (and her cats!) of Earley, Berks. for her photographic expertise and guidance in the production of the photographs in this book. (Also for drawing the seals!).

Authors note

In some photographs of the first *Scillonian* the reader may notice that the ship's rails stretch all the way along the upper deck as far as the very prow of the ship, while in other pictures the vessel seems to have bulwarks stretching back from the prow to a point mid-way between the foremast and the wheelhouse. These were, in fact, heavy canvas 'spray-guards' (for want of a better word) which were attached to the existing rails to provide extra protection for passengers against sea-spray (something to duck behind!), usually during the summer when passengers were more numerous and inclined to promenade on the foredeck. In winter these canvas guards were stowed away, since the first proper wave to hit the vessel would have simply torn them off.

The second and third *Scillonians* never bothered with this arrangement, instead having proper metal bulwarks built into their design in the first place.

CONTENTS

ENA RESEIGH

"…She was also a photographer – not in the professional manner of the Gibson family of Scilly, particularly Frank whose work she greatly admired, but in her own quiet way Ena loved to capture island events whenever they occurred and often tried to create more than just the straight photograph…"

Classic sunset shot over St.Mary's Harbour

Sunlit rollers driving into Porthcressa Bay in 1971

The Isles of Scilly Steamship Company launch *Tean* ashore on Shark's Pit in the mid 1960's having been driven there by an overnight gale. Note the additional mooring ropes attached to the vessel to prevent her being driven further up the beach. She was one of three inter-island launches (the *Gugh* and the *Kittern* were her sister vessels) deployed by the Steamship Company to transport passengers and cargo to the smaller off-islands following their arrival at St.Mary's aboard the *Scillonian*. The salvage job was entrusted to the legendary Matt Lethbridge and so, needless to say, the *Tean* was successfully refloated.

The royal yacht *Britannia* sails out of Scilly with a beautiful Scillonian sunset as a backdrop.

The *RMV Scillonian* just clearing Peninnis on a beautiful, calm day. Quite a good composition this – with the *Scillonian* not being central to the photograph and combined with the expanse of sea this picture emphasises that the ship is embarking on a voyage.

6

Looking back towards St.Mary's from high up on Bryher.

Popular view of St.Mary's Harbour from up near Star Castle – this shot has been one of the classic postcard views of Scilly for decades.

The riot of colour that is Tresco Gardens. Many of the flowers and plants are indigenous to some of the most far-flung and exotic climates of the world and usually don't survive very long when transplanted to the U.K. Here on sub-tropical Tresco though they seem to feel right at home.

One of Tresco Garden's peacocks struts his stuff in front of the ships' figureheads in Valhalla.

Classic shot of heavy seas breaking over the back of the quay – they're about to get a soaking in The Mermaid! Originally a quayside shipping warehouse, it was converted, in 1954, into a public house by the late Rowland Stephenson.

Peaceful late sunset taken from Town Beach, St.Mary's in 1960.

The inter-island launch *Tean* off-loading visitors onto St.Agnes in 1960.

The peaceful scene of St.Mary's Pool in August 1960.

The beach and the road at Old Town torn up by the gales of 1962. Both Old Town and Porthcressa beaches suffered this way over the years until proper sea walls were built.

The *Queen of the Isles* arriving in Scilly in 1966 after what seems, from the look of the sea, like a fairly 'busy' crossing.

Ena Reseigh, the 'Duchess' of Auriga in the back garden of the old Auriga surrounded by the pretty pink of the mesembryanthemum (or 'mezzies' as Ena used to call them).

CHAPTER ONE

ENA AGNES RESEIGH (1906–1981)

THE 'DUCHESS' OF AURIGA

"I done nothing with the kitty!" said the little voice.

Sitting comfortably in an old garden chair in the sun-drenched back yard on this warm, drowsy summer's morning in 1936, Joseph Reseigh, the fifty-one year old skipper of the *RMS Scillonian*, slowly lowered the newspaper he'd been reading and found himself gazing into the face of his four-year old daughter, who was standing alongside the chair with one hand resting on his knee. Her eyes, big, soft brown orbs, stared keenly back at him.

"Say what, dearie?" said the captain, lowering his paper still further.

"I done nothing with the kitty!" reiterated the child, the stare steady and unwavering, the beguiling eyes willing him to believe.

Captain Reseigh yawned, reached awkwardly behind to the Merchant Navy jacket draped over the back of the chair and drew out his pocket watch. Tilting his head to one side and squinting in the bright sunlight, he noted the time – a few more minutes and he'd have to think about heading off down to the quay in preparation for the morning departure of the islands' steamship. Turning his head back towards the house he called out –

"Ena!"

He then looked back quizzically at his daughter for a few seconds before seeming to make up his mind. Levering himself out of the chair, he reached down and took the little girl's hand in his.

"Now then, Jeanne" he said gently, "why don't you show Daddy exactly where you did 'nothing with the kitty'?".

Eagerly, the child led him along the yard to the corner of the old stone-built house where the drainpipe dropped down to, but fell short of, a small mesh grating measuring about six inches square. The captain bent over, peered into the drain and found a pair of round, somewhat baffled eyes staring back up at him to the accompaniment of a faint but plaintive cry. With a sigh, he reached down, lifted the grating to one side and fished out the slightly bedraggled bundle of fur.

"You know, I think he'll be much happier out of there, don't you?" reasoned Joseph, putting the kitten gently down onto the stone path.

"Oh yes," conceded the little girl, "he'll be much happier."

Together, they watched it totter unsteadily off in the direction of the back door, from which a tall, dark-haired woman was just emerging.

In amused tones, Captain Reseigh related the story to his wife as he slipped on his jacket and took the proffered uniform cap from her outstretched hand. He kissed her on the cheek, ruffled his daughter's black locks and strolled off down the path to the back gate. Having watched her husband depart, Ena Reseigh turned and looked fondly down at her first-born. Gently chiding her about kittens in drains and mucky hands, Ena led her daughter indoors to the kitchen, smiling all the while to herself;

"I done nothing with the kitty" she tut-tutted, as she turned the tap on and lifted Jeanne up to the sink where the four-year old began dutifully washing her hands.

The Hicks sisters Ena and Rene aged ten and eleven. Laundry, housework and child-minding were already familiar chores to these young island girls.

Ena Reseigh was a well liked and much respected member of the St.Mary's community in the Isles of Scilly and during her lifetime played a full part within it. A lifelong churchgoer and choir-member of the St.Mary's Parish Church, she also played a major part in running the islands' Brownies and Girl Guide Associations for several decades, becoming District Commissioner in the process as well as being a friend of founder Olave Baden-Powell. A warm and kind-hearted, dignified and gregarious lady, Ena was comfortable in all walks of society, from Buckingham Palace garden party to the local village fete, a quality shared by many of those raised in a truly classless society such as to be found on Scilly. She is probably best remembered, outside her immediate family, as the wife of Captain Joseph Reseigh (skipper of the first Scillonian from 1931–1953) and as proprietress of the guest-house 'Auriga' in Church Street (since re-named Shearwater) which she ran for over twenty years from 1948–1970, before building the present 'Auriga' overlooking Porthcressa in 1970. Here, she continued to take in guests on a reduced scale in what was essentially her retirement home.

Scillonian maid, milkmaid (?!), captain's wife, chorister, Brown Owl, guest-house owner, artist, card and scrabble player extraordinaire, Ena was all of these, as well as being a life-long, benevolently matriarchal figure (never more at home than with an infant child in her arms) to son and daughter, nieces, nephews and grandchildren – and, on the subject of grandchildren, I can safely claim (of course!) that she was the most-fun-to-be-with grandmother of all time! She was also a photographer... not in the professional manner of the Gibson family of Scilly, particularly Frank, whose work she greatly admired, but, in her own quiet way, Ena loved to capture island events whenever they occurred and often tried to create something more than just the straight photograph. The advent of affordable photography for the amateur starting back in the first half of the 20th century and its evolution from black and white prints through to colour slides and later to Standard and Super 8 cine film (Gosh, your own moving pictures!) was as exciting a development in cutting-edge technology then as camcorders and the Internet are today and in a place like Scilly, which lends itself so naturally to the art (ask Frank Gibson!), it's easy to see why Ena, a painter in oils, should embrace photography quite early on in her life.

My grandmother Ena as a teenager alongside her mother, the formidable Bertha Hicks.

Born Ena Agnes Hicks in 1906, Ena Reseigh (it's pronounced Rizz-aaay) was a true Scillonian, an islander born and bred. These days the actual term 'islander' has lost key aspects of the significance that was associated with it in days gone by. Island inhabitants today, as we move into the 21st century, are nothing like as cut off from mainland society as their predecessors were. Nowadays virtually all of modern life's conveniences and creature comforts are taken for granted and one can keep in touch and up to date with the rest of the world (let alone the English mainland) in a nanosecond via TV, mobile phones and the Internet. Even the stretch of water which renders one an islander in the first place is easily traversed, weather permitting, in less than half an hour thanks to helicopters and fixed wing aircraft. Holidays, business trips, even shopping trips are just a phone call away for the modern Scillonian islander with hardships relatively few and far between.

However, the further back in time we go the more the original significance of the word islander becomes apparent. For Ena Reseigh, the Isles of Scilly was the only world she knew for the first quarter of her life. She, like many of her fellow Scillonians of the time, grew up in Scilly and didn't set foot on the English mainland until she was an adult, in her case aged twenty-one. Having never seen that great pioneering British invention the railway, other than in still pictures, Ena could not, at first, be persuaded onto the station platform at Penzance whilst a train was pulling in! Doubtless, other facets of mainland life must have seemed equally daunting during that first, tentative foray away from her safe and, quite literally, insular Scillonian existence.

Insular it certainly was, though, as a large part of the 20th century saw Scilly belatedly catching up with mainland developments. The first telephones started appearing towards the end of the 1930's, taking over from the morse telegraph communications which had existed since the laying of an underwater cable between Scilly and the mainland in 1869. A proper hospital was built on St.Mary's in 1938 and the fixed-wing aircraft service which had been in existence since 1939, mostly with De Havilland Rapide bi-planes, was replaced in 1964 by the Sikorsky helicopter service which still serves the islands today. Some developments were, however, not quite so welcome. The introduction of income tax by the Inland Revenue in 1954 was a bit of a shock to the island community and as for

Maypole flower farmer Alfred Hicks – he built Maypole up to be a successful flower farm on St.Mary's, raised his family of eight children in relative prosperity in times of prolonged economic depression and passed away in his eighties, beloved by his family, in his own armchair in front of his own fireplace – way to go, Sir!

the Government introducing road tax to the islands in 1971 – 'well, what a blooming cheek!' – and with only nine miles of poor roads into the bargain!

Probably the most significant development of the 20th century though occurred in 1920, when the Isles of Scilly Steamship Company was formed and which, a few years later, commissioned the first ship ever to be purposely designed for the rough-water crossing between Scilly and Penzance. Built at Troon in Scotland by the Ailsa Shipbuilding Company and launched in 1926, the *RMS Scillonian*, probably more than anything else, set the islands' modernisation process in motion with a regular service to and from the British mainland and both the islands' flower and tourist industries owe her, and her successors, a major debt. The *Scillonian* also played a great part in my grandmother's life in the years to come.

The early days of Ena's life were spent growing up at Maypole Farm on St.Mary's. One of eight children born to Alfred and Bertha Hicks, her childhood, like that of her sister Rene (pronounced Ree-nee) and six brothers Jack, Leonard, George (who was known as Gee – as in 'G' for George), Lloyd, Joe and Billie, revolved around the

flower-growing that was the family livelihood and part of the, by now, well-established Scillonian daffodil industry. All over the five inhabited islands, these flowers (with names such as Scilly White, Magnificence, Fortune, Golden Harvest and the daddy of them all, the Soleil D'Or) were being cultivated and exported to markets on the mainland, thus providing the main source of income for the islands for many decades. This was all thanks to a gentle climate which allowed for an earlier harvest compared to mainland-grown daffodils, the result being that Scilly virtually created the early market and, consequently, procured the best market prices too – important money for the islanders at a time when the tourist industry had yet to make its real impact on Scillonian prosperity.

At Maypole, all the Hicks children were gainfully employed on the flower farm outside of school hours. In those days, as in many parts of the country, a child was an extra pair of hands and children were a godsend to a farmer – so it was a bonus to have eight of them! Of course, as the only girls in the brood, Ena and her sister Rene's primary responsibilities were fairly obvious – assisting with the raising of six

On an island of flowers – a romance in bloom! The early days of courtship for the sailor and the island girl in the late 1920's outside what used to be The Corner Shop opposite the Scillonian Club. There's no hiding the happiness here!

brothers to begin with; washing, dressing, feeding and generally chivvying them up at the start of each day (you always had to feel sorry for the very youngest – the one that never saw clean bath-water!). Mornings must have been hell:

"Mum, can we go to school now?"

"Are those boys washed and dressed?"

"Yes"

"Have you done the milk round?"

"Er... not yet"

Milk round? Before school? For a 13-year old girl? Yes, dairy cows were a small sideline at Maypole in the early days and before school each weekday morning Ena was obliged to assemble pony and trap, milk churn and ladle and set off to Hugh Town to deliver fresh milk to a number of addresses in town, then return to Maypole (putting away pony and trap) and perform a quick change routine into school clothes before haring off up the road to Carn Thomas School – always late, always ticked off by the teacher. Well, no one said life was easy in Scilly in those days!

Of course, after school there was always time for a bit of recreation except during key harvesting periods. "So what shall we do then? Watch TV? Put a video on? Play on the computer? Text our friends?" Er, no. "We've got beaches though." Then, as now, when you've got a beach to play on you are, in today's horrible vernacular, 'sorted'. Even now we find that if you can put a kid on a beach you can virtually chuck all other toys in the sea (well, almost) and, unlike adults, even the weather doesn't seem to put them off. Thus it was in the old days too and the Hicks children spent many joyful hours swimming, boating and playing games on Scilly's wonderful beaches.

Swimming, in fact, was central to an episode in my grandmother's life which she used as an illustration to her eldest grandson as to why he should never tell lies! (I'd been caught fibbing about something – can't remember what it was but I'll always remember the lesson). Ena's mother Bertha had one day forbidden her daughter to go swimming for some reason or other, although she was allowed to go on a beach picnic with her friends. However, upon seeing the other girls enjoying their swim, Ena succumbed to the temptation and plunged into the sea. Later, upon returning to Maypole, her

1935 Carnival Queen – Ena Reseigh – the two little assistants at her feet are daughter Jeanne Reseigh (right) and June Lethbridge (left), or June Boase as she was then.

mother smelt a rat and challenged Ena as to whether she'd disobeyed her instruction. Unfortunately, my grand-mother elected to deny that she'd been swimming whereupon Bertha, who was quite a bit shorter than her daughter, reached up, grabbed Ena by the ear, pulled her down on a level with her face and licked her cheek! Obviously the salty taste gave the game away and, without further ado, my grandmother received, in her words, "a box round the ears" – not, as it was explained to her, for actually going swimming, but for not being truthful about it afterwards. "So, be sure your sins will catch you out" was the message for me as a twelve year old boy. She was nobody's fool, Bertha, but then I suppose one's elders rarely are!

Life on the flower farm at Maypole in those days was therefore busy and full, what with picking, tying and packing flowers, lifting bulbs from the fields and sorting them, tending the livestock and generally running a farm and a large family minus, of course, most of the labour-saving devices the modern world takes for granted. Everyone had their share of chores and tasks and with the formidable Bertha overseeing everything

I'm fairly sure no one got away with any ducking of their responsibilities! Domestic entertainment at Maypole in the days before television, as everywhere in the country, centred on listening to the radio, reading books or playing board games and, if a house had a piano, there was usually at least one or two members of the family who could bash out a tune if required (and if the others could stand it!). One strange form of domestic enter-tainment unlikely to be found elsewhere occurred when the family were all gathered together up at Maypole to celebrate Christmas one year. An impressive spread had been laid out including a large bowl of jelly, quite an appetising dessert in those days. Realising that there wasn't enough of this tasty dish to go round, one nameless member of the family took his false teeth out and put them into the bowl of jelly saying "That's my bit!". Unfortunately, as most of the family also had false teeth (sad but true!), so each of them entered into the spirit of things and followed suit. The result was a bowl full of false teeth which some bright spark then stirred up with a spoon! How do you then sort out which teeth are whose? What about trying them all until you find a set that fits? (Yuk!).

The Emperor of Abyssinia, a soldierly figure in helmet and cloak, walking through the streets of Addis Ababa, accompanied by his son and attended by his umbrella-bearer.

The real-life Emperor of Abysinnia never knew that for a few hours one day in the 1930's...

...he had a twin brother in the Isles of Scilly! — Ena Reseigh in character at one of the St.Mary's carnivals...

...and who on earth is this? (honestly, grandmothers!)

Joseph and Ena Reseigh on the day of their wedding in June 1930.
Photo: James Gibson.

In the wider community, of course, Scillonians have always been able to make their own (proper!) entertainment, hence the long and colourful history of the St.Mary's Carnivals, May Day celebrations and church and off-island fetes which have continued right through to the present day. In her time my grandmother was herself elected Carnival Queen, a great local honour, then as now, for any St.Mary's maiden. The St.Mary's carnivals have always been quite exotic affairs with their processions of imaginatively-decorated carnival 'floats', while the islanders themselves dress up in costumes depicting all sorts of topical themes. In the 1920's, 30's and 40's, Ena would scour the newspapers and latch onto any public figure that caught her eye as being current at the time. One year she would be dressed up as the Emperor of Abysinnia, the next year she would be the Dalai Lama from Tibet or else a pirate from Gilbert and Sullivan's 'Pirates of Penzance' and, of course, it was pure coincidence that, due to the nature of these personalities, my grandmother nearly always went along to the Scillonian carnivals wearing costumes that inevitably included large, bushy beards!

In her early 20's, Ena met the man she was to marry. Joseph Reseigh, a Mousehole-born man, had recently moved to the Isles of Scilly, having signed up as Mate (second-in-command) on the *RMS Scillonian*. The tall, dark-haired island girl obviously caught the eye of the Merchant Navy sailor, while she, for her part, was charmed by his gentle and modest manner. Each found within the other a kindred spirit, a gentle courtship developed (ahh, the romance of waiting for a ship to dock – be it from ship or from dock!) and in October 1930 they were married. Their first child, a daughter christened Jeanne Mary (mother to yours truly), was born just over a year later and coincided with my grandfather's promotion to captain following the retirement of Captain McAlister, the inaugural skipper of the Scillonian.

This, I should imagine, was quite an idyllic time for Joseph and Ena – for him, a new bride and daughter, his newly-attained captaincy, a new life in the tranquil Isles of Scilly (and no income tax!) while for my grandmother a loving husband (with a key job in the islands), her first baby and a new home 'in town' away from busy Maypole

Proud parents Ena and Joseph Reseigh with their first-born, daughter Jeanne Mary Reseigh (Yes, she is real!).

Farm – and no more milk round! This wasn't the end of her association with Maypole Farm though, as throughout most of her life Ena would return there almost annually during the flower-tying season, a popular way for many of the womenfolk in Scilly to earn a little extra cash – arranging and tying the daffodils into bunches and then boxing them up ready for their journey across the sea to the mainland's markets.

So, peaceful, pleasant times then, when probably the only bad thing ever to happen occurred one day aboard the *Scillonian* when my grandmother was standing on the bridge of the ship alongside her husband. The wind suddenly caught the heavy wheelhouse door and slammed it violently shut on Ena's hand, almost severing a couple of fingers. Hmm... dangerous things, ships.

Along the way, Ena continued her work with the islands' Brownies, ably assisted over the subsequent decades by fellow islanders such as Elizabeth Legg (who started up the Girl Guides later on in 1957), Joan Richards, Diana Phillips and Emily Simpson. The Brownies had been gradually growing in numbers over the years to include most of the island's girlfolk and the 'pack' had become sufficiently significant to warrant being presented to the Prince of Wales during his royal visit to the islands in 1933 – shortly before his abdication as King just three years later!

However, a far darker cloud was looming on the horizon as the world wound its way towards the end of the 1930's and prepared to go to war. For the people of Scilly, in 1939, it must have seemed a doom-laden portent seeing their beloved white *Scillonian* suddenly painted an ominous, brooding black on Admiralty instructions. As the troops, and later on the fighter planes, took up station on the islands, following the outbreak of World War Two, I'm sure the inhabitants of Scilly could only wonder at what might lie in store for them on this far-flung British outpost out in the Atlantic Ocean and close to what were soon to become the U-boat hunting grounds of the Third Reich. Then what would follow? Invasion? A Nazi bridgehead? Look at Jersey and Guernsey. Would Scilly go the same way? Okay, it sounds melodramatic to talk like this now that the history books have been written, but at the time... well, who was to say how it was all going to turn out?

Ena with the islands' Brownies in the 1930's.

Meeting the Prince of Wales during his visit to the islands in 1933.
Photo: James Gibson.

Decades earlier, in 1875, heroic efforts had been made by the Scillonian islanders (particularly the people of St.Agnes) to rescue the passengers and crew of the German ship *Schiller* wrecked one night down amongst the Western Rocks during a terrible storm. The *Schiller* was torn apart by monstrous waves leaving the terrified survivors clinging to wreckage and washed up onto razor-sharp rocks, their cries in the darkness reaching out above the noise of the wind and the seas and spurring their rescuers on to the limits of human endurance as they fought to reach them. It was a long and fearsome night and only a few were ultimately saved but the story goes that the German Government, on hearing of this bravery, vowed never to engage in any future war with the people of the Isles of Scilly.

It's highly unlikely, of course, that Hitler and the German High Command would have honoured this pledge. Had it suited their plans then obviously Scilly could well have gone the way of the Channel Islands. In the event, apart from one or two 'ditched' German bombs, which unfortunately claimed the lives of two civilians, Scilly lived up to its 'nom de plume', the Fortunate Isles, and escaped

Ena Reseigh, broadcasting for the BBC in 1937 as a guest on a famous London radio show called "In Town Tonight" – this particular edition of the show went out on the occasion of the coronation of King George VI.

THE BRITISH BROADCASTING CORPORATION

Broadcasting House, London, W. 1

TELEPHONE : WELBECK 4468   TELEGRAMS : BROADCASTS, LONDON

PROGRAMME DIVISION

Reference PP/AWH.

4th May, 1937.

Dear Mrs. Reseigh,

Mr. Seager tells me that you are coming to London for the Coronation and might be willing to say a few words in one of our "In Town Tonight" programmes next week. We shall be very pleased if you will and I should like you to come and see me as soon as possible after you arrive in London.

I don't know what time your train is due on the 10th, but if it comes in before 6.30 p.m. perhaps you could come straight here.

If the train is not due until later in the evening, will you please come along and see me about ten the next morning?

My wife and I have a great affection for St. Mary's and the other islands. Although we had only a very short holiday it was one of the nicest we remember.

Please send me a line to let me know when to expect you.

Yours sincerely,

A W Hanson

Mrs. Reseigh,
    Auriga,
        St. Mary's,
            Isles of Scilly.

RMC.

Band of Brothers (and two sisters!) – Alfred Hicks senior with his sons left to right Joe, Billie, Lloyd, Leonard and Gee and two daughters Rene (to his right) and Ena. His eldest son Jack was already deceased at this juncture.
Photo: James Gibson.

virtually unscathed from the havoc wreaked in so many other parts of the country.

During this period, my grandmother, now with a baby son named Peter born mid-way through the war, feared for her husband and his crew each time the *Scillonian* set sail for Penzance and the drone overhead of the ship's lone Hurricane fighter plane escort faded gradually away to silence. I'm sure many a quiet thank you was uttered whenever the welcome sound of the vessel's horn signalled her safe return to St.Mary's and, following the cessation of hostilities, it was remembered as a particularly uplifting day in the islands by one and all when the *Scillonian* sailed gracefully into harbour, resplendent in a fresh coat of her familiar white paint and adorned with celebratory flags.

A few years later, in 1948, Captain and Mrs Reseigh moved from Hugh Street to Church Street and the guest-house years at Auriga commenced. For a long time Ena, like many of her fellow guest-house proprietors, offered her guests 'full board' meaning bed, breakfast, packed lunch and evening meal which, as anyone in the hotel and catering business will know, is pretty hard going when you consider it's seven days a week non-stop from April through to the end of September. For many tourist-related occupations there is a 'season' and for most of them, but especially guest-house proprietors, you can safely say they pack a full year's work into that six month period, the more so when you consider most guest-houses are usually one-man (or perhaps I should say one-woman!) operations.

Back then, in the 1940's, 50's and 60's, bed and breakfast establishments were a little more involved than perhaps they are today. With the relative sparsity of inexpensive restaurants, the lack of so-called fast-food outlets and the absence of self-catering accommodation, the guest-house was much more of an all-in deal, more of a home from home and the only real alternative to full-blown (and much more expensive) hotel accommodation.

Auriga offered six bedrooms plus two exterior cabins and could accommodate a maximum of twelve to fourteen guests. With full board plus all the laundry, there was rarely a spare moment once the season was fully underway, even with a bit of extra help provided by the likes of young island women such as Avril Mumford (nee Bell), daughter Jeanne Reseigh or niece Jane Hicks, all of whom helped out variously over the years with a bit of waitressing at meal-times. A busy schedule indeed…

Imagine, if you will, throwing back the covers at seven in the morning, having a quick wash and then heading straight for the kitchen. A dozen packed lunches to be prepared prior to breaking out the frying-pans, ready to cook the dozen or so full english breakfasts that would shortly be demanded, along with the cereals and the endless pots of tea and coffee, all of which had to be traipsed up and down the corridor between kitchen and dining-room. Breakfast through from 7.45 till 9.15, when the guests collect their packed lunches and head off down to the quay, ready to embark on the pleasure boats at 10.15. Then a mass of washing-up to be done (only human dishwashers in those days, of course!), followed straightaway by laying it all out again ready for the evening meal. A quick check and spruce-up of all the guest bedrooms and the bathroom (except on laundry day, of course), grab a quick coffee and then off down to the Co-op and to Woodcock & Mumford, the butchers, to buy all the ingredients for the 2/3 course meal that evening.

Back home and a spot of lunch, then into the

The *Scillonian* photographed from the old quay at low tide.
Not a bad composition actually…

kitchen, washing and preparing the food (no convenience foods, remember, nothing pre-packed and individually-portioned as today) before a couple of hours' respite in the afternoon – and a chance for a quick game of scrabble down on Porthcressa Beach maybe!. Back to the kitchen once more and the hot task of cooking a dozen evening meals, ready to be served from 7pm to 9pm. Another mass of washing-up, then, last thing at night, lay the tables yet again, ready for breakfast the next morning, go to bed and get up the next morning… and do it all over again, seven days of the week for six months of the year. Day off? Not a chance!

After 10,15 or 20 years anywhere in any workplace, we can all of us identify with the sometimes relentless nature of our work – that's why we go on holiday! Still, imagine being surrounded, for six months of the year, by people on holiday – when you're not! Better to be a boatman – wouldn't you say? (they have it so much easier!!).

Certainly my grandmother was pretty exhausted at the end of each year from what was a very labour-intensive occupation. It's taken for granted today but

each new invention on the domestic front turned out to be a godsend during these years – electric kettles, steam irons and automatic washing machines are the obvious examples but how about Tupperware in the early 1960's for those packed lunches? It might seem laughable now but picture it then – new, hygienic, easily-washable and re-useable food and drink containers that were not just waterproof but, more to the point, sandproof – well, these things are important in a place with as many beaches as the Isles of Scilly!

The guest-house years might have been hard and tiring work at times but there were benefits and rewards above and beyond merely making a living. Many of Ena's guests returned again and again to stay at Auriga, as is the case with any good establishment, and over the years a lot of them became lifelong friends with my grandmother, something which brought her much happiness.

Vic Trenwith, the island bus driver, used to drop guests off at Auriga in those days and, if it turned out they were staying at Auriga for the first time, would occasionally, and rather mischievously, inform them that the proprietress was virtually stone-deaf and that they would have to remember to speak loudly and clearly to ensure that Ena understood. Thus my grandmother would look wonderingly at her newly-arrived guests as they traipsed in through the front door of Auriga baying their greetings in her face. Of course, this made Ena assume that **they** were deaf and she would shout back for a minute or two until the penny dropped! Later on, walking up past the Town Hall, she would spy Vic, perhaps leaning against his bus, and hail him: "Vic, I've got a bone to pick with you!" and they would share a laugh about it.

In 1953, Ena Reseigh's life entered its darkest hours when her beloved husband, Joseph, passed away at the age of sixty-eight. Captain Reseigh lost his fight against cancer shortly after surgery at the Royal Masonic Hospital in London and his sudden departing was the cruellest of blows to all of his family but especially to my grandmother, to whom he was everything... the love of her life, the lighthouse that illuminated her path, the compass that guided her... these things and so much more. Widowed at forty-seven. What to do now?

Grief-stricken, my grandmother retired to her bed for several weeks, declining to see any visitors, whether family or friends, while she weathered the emotional turmoil within. Her son and daughter tended her immediate needs while she gradually summoned up the resolve to face the next stage of her life and how she would go about it. I suspect that some key decisions were made at this crossroads…

Many years later in the 1970's, at the age of fifteen, I remember asking my grandmother why she had never re-married. She was writing a letter at her desk in the current Auriga at the time, her reading glasses perched on her nose, and without pausing she simply, and quietly, replied;

"Because I was married to the finest man who ever lived, dear".

It was the way she said it that etched the words forever in my memory – not with impassioned fervour but with the calm sincerity and quiet confidence of someone who truly believed and somehow, even at my tender and insensitive age, I straightaway understood and never had to ask again.

One carries on, of course, and my grandmother took strength from the love she and her husband had shared and this strength sustained her throughout the rest of her life – alone she may have been, if that's possible in Scilly with so much family around, but never lonely – no one ever heard her complain of that. As the years passed by, a pattern emerged whereby, at the end of each summer season at Auriga, and allowing for a few weeks' flower-tying up at Maypole, my grandmother would set off for the mainland and spend two to three months each winter visiting family all over the country as well as staying with some of her Auriga guests-turned-friends. There was always a warm welcome awaiting her wherever she went. To begin with she travelled by train but, in the early 1960's, at the age of fifty-six, Ena passed her driving test and acquired her first car, a white Austin Mini which she christened 'Beauty, Love and Kisses' because of its number plate which ended with the letters BLX.

Passing the official driving test in Scilly has always struck me as being extremely poor preparation for venturing onto the highways and byways of mainland Britain. With no traffic lights, pedestrian crossings, roundabou⋅ or even road-signs on St.Mary's, it's not h⋅ see why one of Ena's sisters-in-law, hav⋅ passed her test in Scilly and deciding ⋅ drive up to London from Penzance o⋅ holiday, got only as far as the firs⋅ roundabout before coming to a dead sto⋅ completely baffled, bless her! She nev⋅ drove anywhere but on Scilly for the rest

"Nan, who's Geronimo?"

The Auriga guest-house in Church Street, St.Mary's in 1948 — here decorated with flags for that year's carnival. Still a guest-house it was re-named Shearwater in 1970 after Ena's brothers and nephews built the third (and present) Auriga overlooking Porthcressa in the same year.

her life! Ena fared somewhat better and, once she'd got the hang of this 'mainland driving lark', there was simply no stopping her! Even the snows of the winter of 1962/3 (when most main roads were deserted) failed to deter her as the plucky little Mini slithered and slipped its way along the A30 from Penzance, amid a total white-out, to reach her daughter's house in Virginia Water in Surrey many, many hours later and in the process notching up a time that wasn't about to grace any record books!

Grandparents can be wonderful things to a child. With the immediate parental responsibility of discipline and up-bringing not quite so much to the forefront, the relationship between grandparent and grandchild offers great scope to indulge in fun and adventure, particularly when you're young and magic is so much more readily conj-urable in the world. My sisters and I had, in the 'Duchess' of Auriga (a title her young grandchildren affectionately ascribed to her), a grandmother who constantly weaved spells with her wand to bring added sparkle to our lives. By the time I was ten years old, we'd had tea with the delightful Lady Baden-Powell, been introduced to the then Prime Minister Harold Wilson (culturally a tad wasted on us at that age, I fear!) and had the fright of our lives in the back of our grandmother's Mini which was being butted by charging reindeer as Ena furiously tried to out-accelerate them on slippery snow-bound roads on the English mainland during the Christmas of 1963 (we'd been feeding these reindeer and had run out of food which they didn't take kindly to!).

Still in the winter of 1963 (Christmas morning, in fact) and I experienced my first car accident at the age of six (incidentally, the only accident I've had where I've not been the one at the wheel!). Ena took me out in 'Beauty, Love and Kisses' on this snowy and very pretty morning and, just over a hundred yards down the road from our home in Virginia Water, there was a long left-hand bend that would have done justice to a corner at Silverstone race circuit. Being a keen, know-it-all driver even at that age I did warn my grandmother about the slippery bend ahead.

"Nonsense", said Ena "my little car doesn't stop for corners."

Of course, your elders are always right and so it was in this case, as the little white Mini skated straight on in one long, glorious slide before vaulting the verge and ending up on its side in the snow-filled ditch, romping along some fifteen feet before finally throwing in the towel and coming to an abrupt halt.

Keen to ensure I didn't become alarmed, my grandmother made light of the situation, laughing and joking as we clambered out of the stricken car. A local farmer arrived with a tractor and, whilst I pompously fielded concerned questions from passing motorists, proceeded to winch the struggling Mini, blushing but undaunted, back onto the road. Grateful thanks were expressed to the kindly farmer and we carried on with our journey – well, we had to get some holly for the tree, I seem to remember!

Some years later and we're on another mission – a secret one this time! Travelling down to Scilly with our grandmother in the early 1970's, my sisters and I found ourselves in Ena's car wending our way through the leafy, tree-shrouded country lanes of the West Penwith peninsula, somewhere 'Away down to Lamorna', as the song goes. A young teenager at the time, I'd recently been captivated by the Derek Tangye books and, knowing of my enchantment with his stories of life, Jeannie, cats and wildlife on the tiny farm at Minack, Ena had planned a little surprise visit to seek out the reclusive author.

"What, to seek out and destroy, Nan?"

"No, dear, we'll just say 'Hello' and maybe have a cup of tea".

Unsure of the exact location (the Tangye's never wanted it to be easily found!) our grandmother, sensing we might be close, pulled over alongside a rugged little stone bridge under which the water sparkled in the haphazard rays of sunlight cutting through the trees, while the stream itself gurgled and splashed its way noisily onto goodness knows where. There, sat on the bridge as if carved from granite himself, was an elderly man, his legs akimbo and his hands resting on the walking-stick poised vertically in front of him – the very picture of peaceful contemplation. Indicating that I should wind down my window, Ena leaned across and hailed him, requesting directions to Minack Farm. Approaching the open window unsteadily, his eyes gleaming, the elderly gentleman started excitedly giving instructions while liberally spraying the interior of the car (and me, of course) with saliva. In the back seat my wide-eyed younger sisters were busy giggling their socks off at this spectacle.

Carnival Queen 1951 – Jeanne Mary Reseigh, daughter of Joseph and Ena Reseigh with assistants Norah Pender to her left and Rosemary Hichens to her right.

"Minack? S'easy, it's easy!" he spluttered, placing one hand on the roof of the car to steady himself. "You go up this 'ere 'ill to the tarp (top!), to the very tarp", he said, wagging one finger in absolute earnest. "When you get to the tarp, you turn left, but..." stabbing the air with said finger in warning, "when you turn left, you don't turn left – you turn roight!", he finished triumphantly.

Thanking the old gentleman most sincerely, we set off for the hill. "Gar! Whatever do you make of that?!", said Ena, her shoulders shaking helplessly with laughter at the seemingly nonsensical directions.

Wonderingly, we continued to the top of the hill and, as instructed, we turned left to find that the road immediately divided into a left and right fork.

"Got it", said my grandmother, as we took the right-hand fork and bumped our way down the tortuous, rocky lane to Minack, grounding the car as we traversed 'Monty's Leap', the little brook mentioned in the stories, on our arrival.

Having read all the books, it was quite magical to turn up and find it was all true and exactly as described. Derek

My grandmother, recently widowed, looks sadly on as the spokesman for the Mal de Mers, a gentleman adventurer's club, dedicates a wooden seat erected on St.Mary's Quay to the memory of Captain Reseigh shortly after his passing in 1953. The seat was later washed away during a storm in the early 1980's which damaged the quayhead and, sadly, was never replaced.

and Jean Tangye were charming and told my grandmother that they lamented the days, many years before, when the *Scillonian* used to sound her horn in salute as she sailed past Minack on her way to Scilly. That gave me an idea and a few years later, in 1977, having kept in touch with the Tangye's, I popped up onto the bridge of the new *Scillonian III* (then in her first year of service) and spoke with Captain Paul Row, her inaugural skipper. Paul listened to my request, dug out the Aldis Lamp and flashed out greetings from the *Scillonian* to those up on the cliffs at Minack as we sailed by. I later heard they were quite touched by the gesture.

The summer of 1969 and a quiet day late in July. It was just after lunchtime at 'Auriga' and Ena Reseigh was busy at work in the kitchen preparing that evening's meal for her clutch of guests when the peace was suddenly broken by the sound of running feet in the hallway and her eleven-year old grandson burst into the kitchen in a heightened state of anxiety.

"Nan! Nan! Uncle Lloyd's punt's ashore on Town Beach and I can't get it back into the water – I don't know what to do!" I exclaimed breathlessly.

My grandmother put down the knife with which she'd been busy peeling potatoes and stared at me.

"What do you mean 'Uncle Lloyd's punt's ashore on Town Beach'?" she said, "What's it doing there?"

Fighting to catch my breath, I tried to explain how I'd 'borrowed' her brother's punt (belonging to the pleasure launch *Swordfish*) in order to practice my rowing out in St.Mary's Pool while all the boatmen were at lunch, how I'd strayed too near the running lines which moor the smaller boats just off Town Beach itself, got entangled in one of them and lost an oar over the side. There was a strong onshore breeze at the time and, with just the one oar, I'd been unable to prevent the boat washing ashore where, try as I might, I just couldn't manhandle the wretchedly heavy thing back into the sea.

"Well, come on then, we can't leave it there, can we!" said Ena, as she undid her 'pinny' and propelled me towards the door, clearly ticked off at this unwelcome intrusion into her busy working schedule.

As we hurried out of Auriga, skirted the Park and made for the Strand, I attempted in vain to justify to my grandmother that it hadn't really been my fault that I'd lost the 'stupid' oar, that 'the wind had suddenly got up', 'the sea had suddenly turned nasty' 'etc, etc, blah, blah, blah'. However, I could see she was unimpressed and I sensed a cuff round the ear looming, so I shut up!

We reached the Rechabite slipway, went down onto the beach and I led my grandmother across the sand to the stricken boat, which was being lapped endlessly at the water's edge by a myriad of fierce little waves whipped up by the stiff breeze.

"Did you manage to recover the oar?" asked Ena.

"Yes, Nan, it's in the boat," I answered.

With that, my grandmother took off her shoes and threw them into the bottom of the punt. She then went round the boat and took the bow in both hands. Hunching her shoulders, she bodily wrenched the boat around, taking three great bites at it, until the bow was pointing seawards, then heaved the boat out into the water until the keel was clear of the sand while I pushed at the stern for all I was worth.

Holding on to the punt, my grandmother waded out into the sea until the water was almost halfway up to her waist, her dress floating around her, then turned and barked at me.

"Well, come on then, get in!"

I was fully familiar with that particular tone of voice and obediently scrambled into the boat without delay.

"Right, help me in," said Ena.

I took an arm and steadied her as she threw one leg over the gunwhale and, with some difficulty, clambered over the side and into the boat. We quickly unshipped the oars and dug the blades deep into the water before the punt could drift back ashore.

With two of us rowing, it was only a matter of minutes before we were safely back over at the Old Quay. We drew alongside and I kept the punt steady as my grandmother clambered out and beckoned for me to hand her the painter (mooring rope). Grabbing her shoes from the bottom of the boat, I scampered up behind her noting the wet footprints her stockinged feet were leaving on the dry stone steps while the sea-

May 27th 1965   Olave Baden-Powell

"Okay, everyone, spot your mums!" The massed ranks of the Isles of Scilly's Brownies and Girl Guides photographed by Frank Gibson on the occasion of a visit to the islands in 1965 by founder Lady Olave Baden-Powell. Today the good work is carried on by Lesley Thomas (Guide Commissioner), Lisbet Jackman and Beryl Read.

In the Westward TV studios in Plymouth in the late 1960's for the programme 'Family Circle – The Hicks family of Scilly'. Facing the camera left to right are Barbara and Billie Hicks, Laurel and Gee Hicks (Gee, as ever, causing mirth with his laconic, dry sense of humour!) and Ena Reseigh while opposite sit Sue and Lloyd Hicks next to Gee's son Michael Hicks. Presenter Guy Thomas looks suitably amused.

water dripped from her sodden dress. Pulling the punt along behind her, she walked a little way along the quay before deftly securing the painter to one of the mooring rings embedded in the stone with a round turn and a couple of half-hitches.

"I didn't know you knew about knots, Nan," I said admiringly, as I studied her handiwork.

"What, you think I've lived all my life in Scilly without knowing how to tie up a cussed boat!" she exclaimed in exasperation.

"No, Nan" I replied sheepishly.

With Scilly as a backdrop, there were plenty of other moments when Ena's sense of fun, mishap and adventure came to the fore. One hot summer's day, during a picnic on the beach, she decided the sea really looked too inviting to resist and, despite literally not having been swimming for decades (probably since getting her ears boxed all those years earlier!), my grandmother took the plunge – fully clothed incidentally as there'd been no swimming costume in her wardrobe since the war. This became a regular event although she, like many bathers in Scilly's chilly waters, disliked walking into the sea and gradually submerging as it gave her the chance to change her mind. Her preferred method was for someone to row her out some way from the shore and then deliberately capsize the boat, pitching her into the sea so that she could enjoy the swim back! I'm sure the sight of a sixty year old lady emerging from the sea wearing a dress and a straw hat must have made more than a few holidaymakers ponder the sanity of the locals and it wouldn't have surprised me if one or two of them even wondered if she'd actually fallen overboard from some passing vessel – which, in some ways, she had!

In 1969, Ena put her retirement plans into action. The second 'Auriga' in Church Street, with its six bedrooms spread out over three floors,

had been physically taking its toll on my grandmother, now sixty-three, for a number of years by this point. In fact, to accommodate all her guests and family descending on Scilly she had, on a number of occasions, spent entire summers sleeping in a bed she'd made up in the garage at the foot of her garden, sometimes accompanied by a handful of huge spiders who would find their way in – usually after a heavy downpour – much to her grandchildren's horror!

"That's alright, I don't take any notice of them and they don't take any notice of me," was her answer to our protestations!

Ena even had a 'pet' seagull called Clarence, a stroppy and territorial 'master of the roof', who enjoyed a cooked breakfast (well, bacon rinds and scraps) every morning in between seeing off all the other feathered 'would-be' diners.

In the end, however, it was all becoming just a little too much. "Time for a bit of a rest," Ena reasoned. "Time to put one's feet up and enjoy taking it easy for a change" – and rightly so.

That year, my grandmother commissioned her brothers, Joe and Gee Hicks, and her nephews, Bennie and David Badcock, to build the third 'Auriga' at the foot of her existing back garden and overlooking Porthcressa Bay. Completed in 1970, this was a smaller, modern and much more manageable dwelling and had been specifically designed to take the utmost advantage of the panoramic vista no more more than twenty-five yards away. Not only did the master bedroom look out over Porthcressa but the upstairs lounge did too. That uninterrupted view of the bay, including those beloved *Scillonians* which, since 1948, Ena had always enjoyed watching as they sailed past, was still hers! This new 'little' Auriga suited her needs admirably and made her very happy in the autumn of her years.

Like the previous Auriga (and indeed like most Scillonian homes), there continued to be an 'open door' policy with everyone and his auntie popping in for a chat on their way through, thanks to the convenient location of the house. Evenings, after choir practice or church, often saw brothers and sisters, nieces and nephews gathered together to spend the evening playing cards, board games or enjoying one of Ena's impromptu cine film and slide-shows (the photographs in this book are but a selection). For those staying at Auriga, there was the indefinable pleasure of the short walk from the front door to the beach to drink in the early-morning or late-evening splendour, peace and tranquility of Porthcressa Bay.

One day, I wandered into the kitchen at Auriga and found my grandmother kneeling on the floor with the door of the big corner cupboard open in front of her. She was holding a loo roll in one hand. I knew she always kept a larger-than-necessary stock of loo rolls at the bottom of this cupboard (a throwback to the days of multiple guests in the older, bigger Auriga) but this particular roll she was staring at very intently indeed.

"What's up, Nan?" I enquired.

For an answer she held the loo roll out. Taking it, I turned it over and saw that almost a third of it was missing. It was all tattered and torn and, on closer inspection, it looked to me as though dozens of tiny little teeth had been at work.

"Gosh, what's going on here?"

"Well, obviously there's a mouse living somewhere behind the back of the cupboard," Ena replied, "and he's managed to nibble his way through and get at the toilet rolls".

"Oh, is that what it is?" I said, still examining the roll of tissue. "But why would a mouse eat toilet paper?" I then stupidly asked (so much for a grammar school education!).

At this, my grandmother shot me a just-ever-so-slightly withering look.

"He's not eating it, dear" she explained patiently, "He's been building a nest with it somewhere – using it for bedding, the blighter".

"Oh, right," I said. "Yeah, blighter".

"Fiddlesticks! Here's another one." my grandmother exclaimed, fishing out a second and passing it to me before delving further into the cupboard. It was in the same condition as the other one.

I was about to say something when out came another loo roll, then another and suddenly I was witnessing the extraordinary sight of my grandmother deep in the cupboard on all fours, chucking out loo roll after loo roll until there must have been nearly a dozen rolling around the kitchen floor. They had all been savaged by the mysterious, miscreant rodent and, from inside the cupboard, I could hear my grandmother muttering away crossly to herself;

"Cussed mouse!" she kept saying, "Cussed, cussed mouse!"

Yes, loo rolls apart, the new Auriga was working out just fine. Ena even managed to hang on to her garage (though no longer for sleeping purposes!). Built into the house it had the unfortunate disadvantage of being at right angles to the very narrow Porthcressa Road and thus required great dexterity on the part of the driver to manoeuvre a car both in and out – something my dear grandmother never quite fully mastered. Often she'd come marching into the house furious with herself.

"Darn it. I've scraped the car again!"

Snow on a palm tree outside the Auriga guest-house
— you see, Scilly does have everything!

Ena Reseigh's retirement home — the third Auriga was completed in 1970 and is still a guest-house today.

As a car-mad teenager, I'd sigh inwardly and slope off to inspect the damage myself, ruefully reflecting, as I examined the bronze flanks of her latest car, that this was becoming more scratchwork than paintwork as time went by!

Time, unfortunately, does go by and tragically, in 1978, Ena suffered a severe stroke which left her partially paralysed. This required my grandmother to forsake her beloved Auriga and take up residence in St.Mary's Hospital for the last few years of her life. All her family visited her and on many occasions took her out in her car around the island, stopping off to play scrabble or cards while looking out over Old Town Bay, Shark's Pit or Porth Hellick – or, indeed, any of her favourite beauty spots. On good days her spirit was as redoubtable as ever, witness the time her nephew John Hicks (skipper of the *Swordfish II*) took her out one day for the afternoon during which a call of nature needed to be answered. With no wheelchair in the car John was all for returning to the hospital. My grandmother, however, would hear none of it and insisted she be taken up to her sister-in-law Sue Hicks' house at Longstone where the lack of a wheelchair was resolved, at Ena's own suggestion, by the improvised use of a wheelbarrow to ferry her, laughing all the way, into the house! Problem solved!

Sadly, but in many ways a merciful blessing, Ena Reseigh finally passed away in 1981. Her daughter Jeanne had become restless about her mother's situation in the November of that year and, despite endless reassurance from the hospital staff that Ena's condition hadn't changed, Jeanne travelled down to Scilly to be with her. This was intuition taking charge Staying at Auriga, she visited the hospital every day for about a week before one day asking the staff if she could stay overnight at the hospital A bed was made up for her and that first night Jeanne went to her mother's bedside just after midnight. Within the hour Ena died.

There were two important birthdays in Ena's life at this time of the year. She had just celebrated her daughter's birthday on November 17th and her beloved late husband Captain Joseph Reseigh had been born on November 19th. The 'Duchess' of Auriga departed this world on the 18th...

"To live on in the hearts of those we love is not to die."

Photography in Scilly – not always as easy as you might think! (Ena Reseigh both behind and in front of the lens on this occasion).

Ena Reseigh and her cousin Eileen Cope at Higher Town, St.Martin's with behind them the perfect arc of one of the most beautiful beaches in the islands.

Sunset over Samson taken from the Garrison.

1966 and Prime Minister Harold Wilson leaves the bridge of the *RMV Scillonian* (escorted by Captain John Thomas) having arrived for one of his many holidays in the Isles of Scilly. The idea of a world leader walking around these islands in shorts and protected only by a couple of plain-clothes officers and a friendly old labrador would have shocked an organisation like, for example, the United States' Secret Service – but then that's Scilly for you! Also in the picture is a young Roger Thompson emerging from the wheelhouse.

Vic Trenwith – lone clifftop bugler, bus driver, island coach tour guide extraordinaire and (along with Richard and June Lethbridge, Maggie Perkovic 'et al') one of the legendary and much-loved 'Scillonian Entertainers'. Always full of fun, Vic loved being on stage, loved being 'on show' and couldn't resist playing to the camera – so trying to take a straight photograph of him could sometimes prove...er...difficult!

Wilfred Tonkin – the fondly-remembered one-legged town crier in Church Street, St.Mary's in 1961. With a cleft palate, a withered arm and minus one leg Wilfred wasn't dealt the fairest of hands in life, bless him, but he carved his niche in the St.Mary's community and won a place in the affections of Scillonians and visitors alike. He also had the right pair of lungs for the job!

The genial disposition of Lt. Cmdr. Tom Dorrien-Smith (Lessee of Tresco and a descendant of the original Lord Proprietor of the Isles of Scilly Augustus Smith) on display here on the occasion of one of his much-loved Tresco fetes in the early 1960's.

Having deftly given her girl guides the slip, Lady Baden-Powell enjoys some relaxed and contemplative moments afforded by the peace and tranquillity of Tresco's Abbey Gardens – this during her visit to Scilly in 1965, where she was a guest of her friend Mary Gillett.

The royal yacht *Britannia* moored in the Roadsteads during one of her visits to Scilly – the light blue vessel in the foreground is the *Sapphire* owned jointly by Bennie and David Badcock prior to their acquisition of the *Guiding Star* and the *Britannia* – no, not this *Britannia*!

The Queen Mother leaving St.Mary's Parish Church, alongside the Reverend James 'Jimmy' Gillett and his wife Mary, during her royal visit of 1962.

The bows of the royal yacht *Britannia*.

Traditional shot of the Bishop Rock lighthouse before the helicopter landing platform was added.

In the days when lighthouses were inhabited. Perhaps they'd make good holiday homes these days — talk about getting away from it all!

Flower-tying in Scilly – like flower-picking, this requires deft fingers if you're not to get left behind. Barbara Hicks, Dot Elvin and Ena Reseigh keep busy up at Maypole Farm. A life-long flower-tyer, Ena could top out at 130 bunches an hour – pretty good going. The average figure is around 85–90.

Island-grown daffodils formed the mainstay of the islands' economy for many decades until superceded by tourism. Latterly picked in bud, these blooms are obviously not for market but make a fine sight nonetheless.

The early 1950's and Briar Hepworth, Margaret Hepworth and Jeanne Reseigh pose for what would now be called a magazine photo-shoot for an article on the islands' flower industry.

A neck-scarf was never mandatory attire for flower-tying on the islands!

That adventurous little Mini of Ena's, adjacent to the Park on St.Mary's when the snows of the harsh mainland winter of 1962/3 reached even Scilly's temperate shores.

Dolphins at play in the waters off Scilly.

The *Waratah* beached on Porthcressa in 1964 after she started taking in water off Scilly. Matt Lethbridge gave assistance in the JML towing her hard into Porthcressa Bay to give her sufficient momentum to run ashore (and allow Matt to swing the JML away at the last second!). She was pumped out, patched and towed round to St.Mary's Harbour.

On display outside the Town Hall – one of several bronze cannon salvaged from the wreck of *HMS Association* in 1967.

Sunset over the twin hills of Samson.

The young Merchant Navy sailor.

25W, but with the Cornish range always aglow there was a warm, dreamlike cosiness to the place which was soothed further by the soft, lazy tick-tock of the old-fashioned clock. I remember that my young sisters were particularly enthralled by the fact that Auntie Janey only ever washed her hair once a year – 'after spring-cleaning' as she put it. This sounded dire to us although, since she wore her hair pinned up in a bun during the day, we could never really be sure about this. However, Mum told us that each night Auntie Janey would undo the bun, let her hair down and brush it out the classic one hundred-odd times when she went to bed and, in the morning, do the same thing before putting it up again. This, rather than washing, was what apparently kept her hair clean. Years before when our mother, a young girl then, had lived with Auntie Janey for a while she used to help brush her aunt's hair (nearly three feet long when it was let down) and Mum assured us it was soft and clean like pure silk.

"You could have lined a baby's cot with it." she said.

Back to the 19th century though and baby Joseph's cot was a drawer in a chest of drawers in his mother's bedroom (though I'm sure he was a top-drawer baby!) before he later moved to a slightly larger 'billet' at the bottom of a wardrobe. So, by the time he elected to pursue a sea-going career at the age of fifteen it's fair to say he'd probably outgrown the family home!

Going to sea was the obvious choice for many young men reared along Britain's coastline. In those days, Britain was still in her prime as a maritime nation and her coasts were probably as busy with a multitude of different vessels then as her motorways are with vehicles today (er, actually perhaps not!). Aside from fishing, of which there was certainly a lot more than today, a surprising amount of mainland produce was transported around the country by sea and young Joseph's early Merchant Navy career took in stints aboard coastal colliers and the like before embarking into deeper waters with an enlistment aboard his first serious vessel, a ship named, intriguingly enough, the

The start of something – Mate Joseph Reseigh and veteran mariner Captain Neil McAlister aboard the fruits of the proud islanders' efforts, the *RMS Scillonian*, on the occasion of her maiden voyage. The date is February 2nd 1926 and they look ready…

The *Scillonian* prepares to come alongside the quay at St.Mary's.

At the helm of the *RMS Scillonian* in those early days.

S.S. Auriga, in recognition of the constellation (also known as The Charioteer) above the Northern Hemisphere. This is why there is a guest-house on St.Mary's in Scilly called Auriga, the third house to bear the name incidentally, and a legacy from that first foray into the world's oceans in the early 1900's.

The sea represented a calling for many of Joseph's family. His brother Obed (this unusual name was to run through three Reseigh generations) also went to sea and found his niche aboard the deep-sea yachts of the wealthy gentry, while first cousin Robert Hichens found more notoriety than fame in his maritime career when, a quartermaster at the time, he found himself desperately hauling the helm hard over aboard the pride of the White Star Line to avoid an iceberg one fateful night in April 1912. Having survived the sinking of the *Titanic*, he ended up in South Africa where he made quite a bit of money selling his survival story to the newspapers but later on, following his return to England, he ended up in prison for a year following some shady boat deal or other. Oh dear – the ups and downs of fame and misfortune!

By the time the Isles of Scilly Steamship Company had been formed by the enterprising Scillonian islanders in 1920, Joseph Reseigh had acquired nigh on twenty years' sea-going experience on a variety of Merchant Navy vessels. Along the way he had also been married and widowed, tragically early, but not before fathering three children – two sons, named Francis and Obed, and a daughter named Muriel. Francis and Obed both went into the Navy and, in fact, Francis Collingwood* Reseigh became one of the last naval ratings to

* 'So-named in recognition of Admiral Cuthbert Collingwood (1750–1810), who, aboard *HMS Royal Sovereign*, headed the second of the two lines of Royal Navy ships which breached the combined broadside fleets of the French and Spanish navies at the Battle of Trafalgar. Admiral Nelson, of course, headed the other line of ships aboard *HMS Victory*, but Collingwood's faster vessel reached the enemy before *Victory* and drew first blood, much to Nelson's admiration. Although not an adventurous risk-taker like Lord Nelson (and vastly overshadowed by him as a heroic public figure back in England), Collingwood was, nevertheless, a formidable naval commander held in extremely high regard by both sailors and Admiralty alike. His death, in 1810, from ill-health aboard the ship *Ville de Paris* while blockading an enemy fleet in Port Mahon, was a direct result of the Admiralty's refusal to accede to his request to be allowed to return home – on the grounds that his services were indispensible. A worthy, alternative hero to Horatio Nelson (Horatio and Cuthbert? Come on, don't you just love those names!).'

Captain's son no.1 – Commander Frances Collingwood Reseigh RN. had a distinguished lifetime career in the Royal Navy. His grand-daughters Button (christened Jane) and Beth (daughters of John Reseigh) together with Button's partner Gaz today run the small cafe 'Dibble & Grub' overlooking Porthcressa Beach.

Captain's son no.2 – Obed Reseigh. Another naval officer (a petty officer in this photograph) Obed left the navy and disappeared out into the wide world. Sadly, we never knew what became of him.

Captain's daughter no.1 — Muriel Reseigh, a life cut tragically short.

Captain's daughter no.2 — Jeanne Mary Reseigh. Scillonian-born in 1931, Jeanne ran her late mother's guest-house overlooking Porthcressa from 1985 until her own untimely passing in 2000, at the age of 68. Captain Reseigh also passed away aged 68, as did Augustus Smith, the original Lord Proprietor of the islands — so, at least, Jeanne was in good company on that score…

Captain's son no.3 – Peter Reseigh, himself a Merchant Navy officer, boards the *Scillonian* at St.Mary's in 1961, following leave spent with his mother at Auriga.

Sitting on the wall outside the cottage at Mousehole – the author, his sisters Joanna Mary and Sarah-Jayne together with Auntie Janey, Captain Reseigh's sister and inheritor of his birthplace.

work his way up the ranks, from 'bilge to bridge' as it were, finishing up as a Royal Navy Commander at the height of his career. Obed cut short his naval career and, never really finding his true metier outside the Navy, he eventually disappeared into the wide world, sadly never to be seen again. Joseph's daughter Muriel married Lloyd Hicks of Scilly (for so many years the skipper of the St.Mary's launch *Swordfish*) but tragically, in 1945, poor, gentle Muriel died at the early age of thirty from cancer.

In 1926, Joseph Reseigh procured the post of Mate (first officer to the skipper) aboard the Isles of Scilly Steamship Company's vessel *RMS Scillonian*. Sometime, during the next four years, he met and wooed my grandmother Ena Hicks, as she was then, and they were married in 1930. In their first year of marriage Joseph's new bride accompanied him when he went 'up country' to Liverpool to study for his master's ticket, as it was known. A year later, in 1931, he succeeded Captain Neil McAlister as master of the *Scillonian* and became a father again with the birth of my mother Jeanne (an original captain's

daughter if ever there was one*) – so, a good year all round! Thus, with this latest promotion, began the association which saw Joseph Reseigh dedicate the rest of his professional seafaring life to serving the islands' community as captain of their proud ship. He did this by dutifully maintaining the vital social and economic link between the Isles of Scilly and mainland Britain that the *Scillonian* represented then and, through her later incarnations, still represents today. During those twenty-seven years' service (twenty-two as Master), Captain Reseigh's devotion to duty led to him becoming one of the islands' best-loved skippers and he was still commander of the vessel when he passed away at the age of sixty-eight in 1953.

The inhabitants of the Isles of Scilly did well, back then in 1920, to launch their own steamship company. They did well to launch their first purpose-built ship a few years later in 1926. However, I think the real success story lies in the fact that they kept the whole shooting match afloat at all. After all, they could hardly have chosen a worse economic climate in which to 'go it

*Nothing to do with saucy limericks! Spirited, adventurous, outgoing and gregarious, Jeanne shared her parents' love of people, loved her island home and upbringing, loved ships, boats and being on the water (also loved driving fast cars fast – but that's another story!).

Blurred view of Mousehole Harbour taken through the thick glass window of No.7, Fore Street in the 1960's – the cottage where Captain Joseph Reseigh was born and grew up.

R.M.S. "SCILLONIAN" ARRIVING IN A GALE. NO.189.

The *RMS Scillonian* arriving in Scilly during a gale. In those days such weather was just part and parcel of the 'mission'.
Photo: James Gibson.

Captain Reseigh with war-baby son Peter.

alone' after decades of chartering vessels. The country was in the throes of economic depression, 1926 was the year of the General Strike, unemployment was rife and there was to be no quick turnaround by somehow magically kickstarting Britain's economy. The lean years were to continue well into the 1930's and only hard work would enable any new company to survive its gestation period at such a time. Fortunately, Scillonians are a hardy breed and, to be honest, having undoubtedly faced tougher challenges in the islands' past, they weren't about to shy away from this latest one. More to the point, they now had, with their shiny new vessel floating alongside St.Mary's Quay, the right tool for the job – one which was capable not only of helping with the islands' economic survival but also of being instrumental in their journey towards prosperity. All it would need was willpower and perhaps a touch of that mystical good luck that the Fortunate Isles have somehow always been able to conjure up just when it's needed most. The *RMS Scillonian* would certainly not be sitting around gathering barnacles on her bottom in port. From the very

beginning she was on a crusade!

On February 2nd 1926, as she embarked on her maiden voyage, Captain Neil McAlister and his second-in-command Joseph Reseigh both knew full well the importance of the *Scillonian*'s mission. This ship had to go to sea at all times. It was in everyone's interests that she did – in fact, livelihoods depended upon it. Island produce, whether cut flowers or vegetables, was of no good to anyone sitting around in containers on quaysides in the days before refrigeration and 'sell by dates'. A day or more's delay during that crucial period when mainland market prices were falling could mean far more than just the difference between butter and 'dripping' for the island children sitting around the breakfast table each morning. Holidaymakers, then relatively few in number but gradually increasing year by year, had to be returned to the mainland on time. Forty miles away in Penzance lay the freight cars and passenger coaches of the Great Western Railway ready to hold up their end of

Work being carried out on the *Scillonian* in 1930 while she was laid up in dry-dock in Newport.

This was some re-fit with plates replaced both above and below the waterline.

A little welding just ahead of the prop. (The gentleman onlooker is very possibly Mr. Fred Ward, the inaugural chairman of the Isles of Scilly Steamship Co.).

Old skills at work – riveting new plates onto the *Scillonian's* hull below the waterline.

Mate Joseph Reseigh gets 'hands-on' aboard the *Scillonian* during her time in Newport.

The kindly face of Captain Neil McAlister, the inaugural skipper of the *RMS Scillonian*. This vastly-experienced sailor concluded his maritime career by captaining her from her maiden voyage in 1926 until his retirement from the seas in 1931.

Being presented to the Prince of Wales in 1933.
Photo: James Gibson.

the transport deal – carrying goods to market, thus securing the islanders' income, and returning tourists to their homes in the hope they would spread a good word about the beautiful Isles of Scilly amongst their friends and acquaintances and thus encourage others to venture to these far-flung islands. The ship MUST sail!

It might not have seemed so then, with unemployment such a constant threat to one and all, but, with hindsight, it was, perhaps, one of the more rewarding eras in which to be captain of the *Scillonian*. During these times, with the absence of modern navigational aids such as radar, echo-sounders, GPS and the like, the human qualities of skill, experience and judgement counted for everything and the position of master mariner was something won, on absolute merit, the hard way – not in the classroom, but after years of graft in an uncompromising arena.

In addition, the new vessel really was the only means of maintaining the link with the mainland, the only real way forward for the islanders of the time and so it was make or break for the fledgling steamship company. Elsewhere, in the maritime world, qualified captains were reduced to earning peanuts as deckhands and so here was a rare gauntlet of opportunity thrown down to those quick enough (and with the necessary determination and commitment) to pick it up and run with it.

Meanwhile, in this leaner, more spartan era, the first *Scillonian* was equipped with all the latest technology of the day – a compass and a plumb-line! That was it, although she was later fitted with a ship-to-shore radio-telephone. I often find myself wondering how the skippers of that generation would view the current maritime scenario. With all the modern navigational aids at our disposal today, would they not be baffled at how many vessels still manage to come to grief all over the world as we lurch into the early part of the 21st century? Witness the *RMS Mulheim*, wrecked at Land's End during the winter of 2002/3, or

the Royal Navy destroyer *HMS Nottingham* which came close to foundering after hitting a rock off the Queensland coast of Australia last year. Perhaps, on reflection, those 'ancient mariners' would smile ruefully, recognizing in their wisdom that nature and the elements will, in the end, always have their say whenever they suspect Man to be guilty of underestimating them!

Sound judgement has always been a pre-requisite of the role of master mariner but in those days the captain was entrusted with a touch more of the final say in matters regarding his ship. In modern times there's a plethora of regulations to do with EU rules on health and safety, corporate liability and possible litigation (not to mention modern business economics), all of which means that some of the key decisions now take place in the Company boardroom and not under the captain's cap. The Board of Trade, as it was known in those days, laid down certain regulations and criteria for the building of ships but the responsibility (and the risk!) thereafter lay almost exclusively with the captain of the vessel.

This is not to impugn the skill of modern mariners by any means, but it's fair to say that the creeping tide of bureaucratic and, in some ways, technological 'interference' has been steadily eating its way into what has traditionally always been their territory and eroding some of the older-style challenges faced by their forebears – but then, alas, many professional walks of life have felt this 'pinch'. For example, airline pilots I have spoken to at Heathrow Airport have been united in lamenting the passing of Concorde, since what remain in our skies are

essentially computer-designed and controlled fly-by-wire creations flown by pushing buttons and entering data, whereas our graceful, beautiful and exquisitely-engineered supersonic triumph was a hands-on, gut-instinct, seat-of-the-pants machine – think Ferrari or Aston-Martin of the skies (then multiply by ten!) – a true flyer's aircraft.

Returning to the world of ships, each of the three *Scillonian*s to date have had their admirers and their detractors but, in terms of design, the first *Scillonian*, despite being the smallest at 453 tons (and the slowest at 12 knots!), was probably the purest of the three ships built so far. Apart from being able to carry both passengers and cargo, there were two key criteria within the ship's design brief. Firstly, she had to be able to negotiate the very shallow waters within the islands which put a natural limit on the amount of water she could draw both at low tide and when fully laden. Secondly, she had to be built to withstand the sort of rough weather to be found in that stretch of water between Land's End and Scilly where the sea, at times, can truly get serious. With most of the mechanical hardware within her hull below the waterline and with relatively low superstructure (and not that much of it), the *RMS Scillonian* was a tough, sturdy and reasonably stable little ship well suited to her task and lacking only the modern stabilizers that the more recent vessels rely on to provide passenger comfort while underway at sea. Her successors, though worthy in their ability to meet their respective commercial challenges and undoubtedly offering much-improved passenger facilities, have gradually been compromised more in sea-going terms by the increase in their size which has not, for obvious reasons, been accompanied by a corresponding increase in their draught, or at least not to the extent truly desirable.

The second vessel to be built, the *RMV Scillonian*, came into service in 1956, weighing in at some 900 tons with a speed of 16 knots, while today's *Scillonian III*, bless her, weighs 1200 tons, can do 21 knots (though usually cruises at 17 or 18) but draws only 9 feet (the first *Scillonian* drew 10) and reminds me somewhat of a World War Two Royal Navy destroyer gamely trying to nail a German U-boat whenever she heels over on the turn-in towards St.Mary's Quay! That said, *Scillonian III*, like her two predecessors, has provided a solid and reliable service since her launch in 1977, although in recent years she has found herself, for financial reasons, laid up in Penzance during the winter months in a slightly ignominious end to her annual season. Such are the economics of modern business that, sadly, she is no longer the brave, year-round, all-weather mariner she once was. Nevertheless, *Scillonian III* remains for many people (myself included) the only 'proper' way to travel to and from the Isles of Scilly. Maybe one day she'll make her return to the wild winter seas…

I'm sure this doesn't really sit well with her current master, as sailors, particularly Cornish-born sailors, traditionally don't enjoy whiling too much time away in port and the Isles of Scilly Steamship Company has always chosen well in securing the services of skilled masters over the years. From captains McAlister and Reseigh in the early days, through captains such as Daniel, Thomas, Davies, Evans and Kemp, to the latter day skippers Paul Row and David Pascoe (along with Mate Peter Crawford), the masters and their crews have always dedicated themselves unfailingly to the task in hand, knowing how much the islands depend on them.

What all three *Scillonians* have always been able to offer is the magic and romance (the occasional sea-sickness aside!) of that first-ever trip for the first-time visitor to the Isles of Scilly. Evelyn Waugh, among others, wrote that fully to appreciate Venice one has to make the approach by sea and the same, I feel, is true of the Isles of Scilly. If at all possible, choose a fairweather day and enjoy the leisurely pace (do we really need ever more speed in life?) as the *Scillonian* glides along the twelve miles of rich and rugged coastline between Penzance and Land's End, picking off key coastal landmarks as she goes... the famous Penlee lifeboat station, Mousehole, the Tater Dhu Light, Lamorna Cove. As she clears the Land's End peninsula, wander towards the *Scillonian's* stern, settle yourself into one of the seats on her after deck, slowly sip something native to the region (a rum and shrub perhaps!) and contemplate your country. Looking back at Land's End it is easy to picture Britain as the island she is when the Atlantic Ocean itself divides at this very point. Close your eyes and feel the sun's rays blessing your face, savour the sea air on your lips and reflect on the busy pace of mainland life that you have been wrestling with up until now. Celebrate the moment, this ritual act of purging the stresses and strains of modern existence, feel them slowly ebb from your system and enjoy the peace and inner calm which gradually warms and pervades your soul.

Open your eyes and cast your gaze around at the shimmering, expanding ocean, the Longships lighthouse off to starboard, the Wolf Rock lighthouse to port – hmm, I wonder which is taller? Is that a gull or a small plane gliding along in the distance? Difficult to tell how far away it is...

As the toe of England's land mass shrinks away before your very eyes all becomes sea and sky. The engines' beat, muted and metronomic, becomes the clock slowly ticking away time as *Scillonian III* unhurriedly charts the course towards her destination. As the voyage continues, a variety of unrelated thoughts may come and go in your mind before they start to turn collectively towards the focal point of your journey. Curious now, you proceed forward along the deck, eyes searching the horizon ahead for that first glimpse... there, is that something? Yes... yes, definitely.

The low, huddled little mass appears out of the sea and slowly, slowly begins to grow in size. Colours start to form and shapes to evolve. Still the *Scillonian* forges on as the island ahead widens and you realise that it is gradually separating out into several little islands... and then into many little islands, some larger, some smaller, some just rocks. The colours multiply – green for the grass, purple for the heather, yellow for the gorse and beige and grey for the rocks kissed white at their bases by the surf of the iridescent water. The islands open out in welcome, offering up a passage into which *Scillonian III* faithfully turns. The sun-drenched Eastern Isles pass by to starboard, while to port the darker, wooded island which is St.Mary's looks down at you. The ship begins to slow as she swings gracefully to port. You are spoilt for choice now as your eyes struggle to do justice to what's before them. Off to starboard... the long island of St.Martin's, then Tean and St.Helen's with the white dash of Round Island lighthouse behind, Bar Point on St.Mary's off to port. Back to starboard again (Heavens, where to look..!) the lush vegetation of Tresco catches your eye and

1945 and a black-painted *Scillonian* arrives in Scilly decorated with flags showing that, yes, the war's really over!

...and then back in her traditional white.

"Contrary to what many people will tell you, a voyage aboard the *Scillonian* can be highly romantic...... trust me!"
Painting by Jean Blaxall.'

Outside Buckingham Palace on the occasion of receiving his MBE, Captain and Mrs. Reseigh with friend and jeweller Mr. John Bennett.

the beaches... everywhere just beaches... long, clean lines of golden white sand gracing the water's edge with the wild marram grass framing them in an unkempt fringe. Can this really be England?

Throttled back now, the *Scillonian* glides slowly, smoothly, quietly between the islands, feeling in some strange way as though she's no longer touching the water, that she's somehow hovering just above it. The Crow Sound marker slides by, so near, almost, that you feel an instinct to reach out and lay your hand on it, this the closest, most tangible part of the islands for you thus far. Nearby, a brightly-coloured pleasure boat full of suntanned holidaymakers catches your eye. Their happy faces look up and bronzed hands wave at the new arrivals. They know the magic of these islands and they'll happily share it with you now that you're here, though once back on the mainland after their holiday they'll hug it to themselves like some delicious, guilty secret. The suspension of belief is suddenly shattered by the shock of the *Scillonian's* horn as she warns those on St.Mary's Quay of her imminent arrival. The leisurely docking affords you the chance to come to terms with your new surroundings and, once on the quayside, you look back at the little white ship that brought you here. The *Scillonian* somehow looks bigger than she did in Penzance. Here where she belongs, in the little port of St.Mary's, she looks right at home and seems to bristle with all the pride of one of Southampton's finest. There's a clanking hubbub going on as she unloads her cargo but you sense instinctively that just a few yards away you'll find, around the corner and through an invisible wall, a peace and tranquility, a serenity and space that you may never have realised was possible within our shores.

Okay, a touch fanciful, I agree, but it must be something like this because the first thing every boatload of *Scillonian* passengers does, after disembarking at St.Mary's, is promptly to walk (in a state of enchantment perhaps?) down the middle of Hugh Street as if the motor car had never been invented! They're all quite put out when they get hooted at by the first one that comes along.

If you're the type who prefers stormy weather, then to take a trip on the *Scillonian* in the depths of winter would require the services of H.G.Wells' time machine (or perhaps a DeLorean sports car with certain modifications!). If you do go back, pick a worthy date – Sunday 29th December 1935 would be a good one. Enjoy a five hour crossing in the darkness of a hardier age where belief, perhaps, was easier to come by. Stand alongside Captain Reseigh and his crew as they beat through an Atlantic mid-winter storm to deliver a sick islander to a hospital in Penzance. Brace yourself as you stand in the swaying, creaking, wooden wheelhouse of the old *Scillonian* and struggle to sip a scalding cup of tea as, lights dowsed, the crew peer keenly out at the thunderous scene ahead – the blackened, forbidding sky, the forlorn moaning of the wind, the sea-spray curling like icy sleet around the vessel's bows as they alternately lift and plunge through the turbulent sea, while the rain lashes the glass like hail. Feel the low shudder as the hull finds the troughs in the waves and distorts around them. Irrespective of your religion, you may just feel that for the next few hours the Atlantic Ocean itself might be your god or, at the very least, the keeper of your immediate destiny. The steady, relaxed countenance of the crew though comes as reassurance.

"Aye, it's a bit plain today", one of them says and, for a moment anyway, your fears recede as the rugged little steamship battles valiantly on through the elements.

In the wheelhouse of the *Scillonian* in the days before the 'no smoking in the workplace' policy!

If the first *Scillonian* was tough then the same could be said of her crew. Trawling through my grandfather's entries in the *RMS Scillonian's* logbooks, it soon becomes obvious how dedicated he and his crew were. Although the vast majority of voyages were straightforward and passed without incident there are, here and there, examples of a commitment and willingness to put to sea at any time and under almost any circumstance. For example, the aforementioned:

Sunday 29th December 1935:

"1600h. Orders to proceed to Penzance with serious hospital case.

2050h. Landed stretcher case for hospital."

The stretcher case in question was 27 year old St.Mary's farmer Frank Roberts who, six days earlier, had accidentally shot himself in the leg whilst out shooting rabbits near Old Town. In spite of treatment on St.Mary's the patient had taken a turn for the worst and the island physician, Dr.Addison, decided that he needed to be transferred to the West Cornwall Hospital on the mainland.

(In those days, the *Scillonian* was occasionally pressed into service in severe weather where a patient was perhaps too ill to endure a crossing in a smaller vessel. Today, such cases

"What's all the fuss about?" A relaxed pair of sea-dogs, Captain Joseph Reseigh and Chief Engineer Alfred Nicholls, ponder the question as they pose for a newspaper photograph recording their quarter of a million sea miles notched up aboard the *Scillonian*. Over the 27 years they forged a strong, almost telepathic working relationship. 'Alfie' was aboard the vessel right from the start, nursing her through an eventful voyage down from her birthplace in Troon, Scotland and I suspect that it was with a touch of almost parental pride that he used to refer to the *Scillonian* many years later as 'the old girl'.

are usually airlifted to the mainland.)

Or, if you, dear reader, can go the distance on this one!

Monday 10th February 1936:

"0700h. Strong S.E. gale. High seas sweeping over pier. Man standing by to unmoor ship to leave for Scilly.

0800h. Sailing cancelled for a.m. tide. Weather too bad to leave harbour.

1200h. Gale continuing and increasing in force. Ship now aground. Taking on cargo.

1500h. Crew and shoremen mustered and standing by. Extra big rope put out through quarter pipe ashore.

1600h. Ship afloat. All hands standing by onboard and ashore. Steam on main engines and working slow astern to ease after mooring. Gale now increased to hurricane force. Waves sweeping over piers and in harbour. All possible moorings put out, ship pulling and swaying heavily on moorings.

1700h. Starboard after spring parted – removed and secured.

1800h. Parted port mooring aft (chain sling ashore). Renewed and secured.

1910h. Parted again after port wire secured and renewed by rope spring. Hurricane continues, ship rolling and swaying heavily.

2200h. Ship aground. Men released during time ship aground.

0000h. Gale continues S.E.

(Not recorded in the log, but reported in the *Western Morning News*, was the story of the ship's mate Mr.Carson who had a narrow squeak when the ship's gangplank was blown away by the ferocious wind –

with him on it! He ended up in the water between the *Scillonian* and the quayside in a potentially fatal predicament, given the weather conditions at the time, but was quickly plucked to safety by his fellow crew members – that's got to have been worth a drink, lads!)

Tuesday 11th February 1936:

0400h. Gale continuing. All hands standing by as before with engines working slow astern.

0630h. Parted again after chain. Secured and renewed. Nothing further happened this tide.

1030h. Ship aground. Taking on more cargo.

1200h. Weather moderating.

1400h. Crew mustered to clear away broken ropes etc. and prepare ship for sea. Strong E.S.E. wind. Heavy sea.

1730h. Left Penzance for Scilly. Wind now moderate E.S.E.
1800h. Bucks Pt. abm (abeam). S/C (steered course) W x S. Log set.
1832h. Runnelstone abm. S/C W x S. 5.5
1910h. Wolf Rock Lighthouse abm. A/C (altered course) W
10.5 Wind moderate. Heavy sea. Misty.

2020h. Steaming half-speed. Thick misty rain.

2045h. Mist cleared and full speed.

2110h. Peninnis Head abm. Log 32. Half speed through St.Mary's Sound.

2130h. Arrived St.Mary's pier. Light S.E. wind. Overcast.

Commenced working cargo."

In all then, thirty-eight and a half hours to complete a single scheduled crossing from Penzance to Scilly! As if that wasn't bad enough the crew's work wasn't finished until the ship's cargo had been off-loaded. Hopefully there weren't too many fare-paying passengers on this particular trip. Could you imagine the TV 'Watchdog' report today?!

It is often said that in my grandfather's hands the *Scillonian* never missed a trip. This wasn't strictly true as in peacetime an occasional 'no-sailing' would occur with an additional trip hastily pencilled in a day or two later to compensate. Ironically, it was during World War Two that Captain Reseigh performed the laudable feat of achieving almost an exact 100% sailing record for those war years between 1939 and 1945, with just the one sailing cancelled on 17th December 1942 due to exceptionally bad weather (and recorded in a letter at the time from one Vice-Admiral C.H.Pilcher, R.N.) – a service record that contributed to both him and Chief Engineer Alfred Nicholls being awarded the MBE by King George VI.

Another factor in this award was attributable to the stationing, by the War Office, of a garrison of British troops on Scilly throughout World War Two. With Britain's warships obviously in demand elsewhere in the world, the *Scillonian* was pressed into service in ferrying some 40,000 troops back and forth between Scilly and the mainland over the course of the war and, quite obviously, such activity made her a legitimate military target for our German enemies of the time. For this period in her life the *Scillonian* was painted black, her bridge was reinforced and she was fitted with a Lewis gun (later supplemented by a second). She was also provided with a Hurricane fighter plane escort. The Hurricane's mission was obviously one of protection but I can't imagine it to have been the most exciting of postings for the pilots whose RAF buddies elsewhere were busy achieving great things against the Luftwaffe out over the English Channel. This was borne out by a tragic accident which befell one of the Hurricane pilots during the course of 'buzzing' the *Scillonian* by flying between her masts, an activity in which some of the pilots participated – as much to keep their flying skills honed as to relieve the undoubted boredom that escort duty of this type inevitably used to bring about.

Captain Reseigh's log entry for **Thursday August 12th 1943:**

"1135h. Hurricane airplane collided with ship striking fore topmast, crashed into the sea in flames and disappeared from ship on starboard beam. Spent twenty minutes cruising wreckage in lifeboat. Position at time of accident – Lat. 49 degrees, 58' N, Long. 50 degrees 55' W."

Picture the scene: wartime off the Cornish coast and, as yet, a typically uneventful crossing for *RMS Scillonian*, the beat of her engines, thudding quietly away below, overlaid by the gentle hiss of the water slipping along her hull as the vessel steamed south-westwards towards the islands, the faces of those on deck soothed by the warmth of the August sun and the freshness of the sea air. High overhead, the drone of the Hurricane's engine waxed and waned faintly in the distance as the little fighter plane meandered back and forth across the summer sky, her pilot maintaining station with the miniature ship down below whilst keeping a hawk's eye watching brief out over the surrounding scene – ready to peel off in an instant and investigate that speck which suddenly appeared out of the clouds or that glint of something uncertain in the wide expanse of glimmering ocean stretching all around…

The officers and crew of the *Scillonian* looked round lazily at the sound of an engine growling and deepening in volume, as Flight-Sergeant T.B. Hunter dropped the Hurricane down to sea level and into a fly-past which brought his machine low and fast alongside the steamship, his face and raised hand visible just for an instant inside the cockpit and acknowledged by the answering waves of those aboard the *Scillonian*. Skipping just above the waves, the snarling fighter flashed past the ship and lifted slightly as she peeled off into a long, low arc

"Thursday, 12th August 1943 with only seconds remaining for this world for Flight-Sergeant T.B. Hunter as he lines his Hurricane up to fly between the *Scillonian's* masts."
From a painting by Jean Blaxall, commissioned for this book. Jean trained to become an art teacher in the mid–1970's at St.Luke's College of Education in Exeter. She now lives in Australia but, following a childhood affair with Cornwall, repeatedly leaves her heart in Sennen Cove after each and every visit!'

At the helm of the *Scillonian* again — many years later this time!

out across the water, her engine note fading gradually away before solidifying again as she turned and lined up for the dashing manoeuvre that would see her streak straight and true between the needlepoint markers which were the *Scillonian's* twin masts.

Aboard the *Scillonian*, everyone made their way to a suitable vantage point to watch. They'd seen this before, of course, and it was impressive to behold. The Hurricane started to grow in profile out of the sky as she started her run towards the vessel, her speed increasing dramatically as she tracked purposefully across the sea with the *Scillonian's* broadside square in the pilot's sights. A thrill went through those aboard the steamship – a thrill tinged with a slight hint of the sinister. After all, were this a Messerschmitt instead of one of 'our boys' then this might be something akin to how an enemy fighter's attack run would go…

The silhouette of the Hurricane had now started to open out into discernible detail. She was approaching fast, by God, arrow-straight and level and the various noises of the mechanical cacophony that was her engine were beginning to meld and mesh into that gloriously vocal Merlin snarl that every citizen across the country found so uplifting during World War Two. Here she comes…

Heads craned upwards as the Hurricane thundered overhead when… thwack!… just as vibrations from the roaring engine had started sending feelers along the decks of the *Scillonian* and raising hairs on the back of necks amongst those aboard her, there came an ear-splitting crack and, simultaneously, a slight shudder went through the vessel as the *Scillonian's* foremast snapped off, struck by the aircraft's port wing. In that same instant there was a muffled thud as the fuel spilling out of the torn wing of the aircraft flared into a sheet of flame. Heads whipped round in time to see the wounded Hurricane ablaze as the undamaged starboard wing 'powered' itself up and over due to the sudden

imbalance in lift, inverting the stricken aircraft and smacking her hard into the sea, giving poor hapless Flight-Sergeant Hunter absolutely no chance of survival. The hiss from the sea as it swallowed the gallant little downed fighter echoed the hiss escaping from the lips of those who had helplessly witnessed this tragic spectacle, shocked into silence as people always are when the thrill of a joyride turns suddenly and violently into the death knell of disaster.

Despite the search mentioned in the log entry, no trace was found of the pilot and the *Scillonian* had to continue her journey to Scilly and report this sad event on arrival.

Over the years, ever since my grandmother first related this story to me when I was a small boy, I've often wondered (and to a degree worried) about Flight-Sergeant T.B. 'Johnny' Hunter. Irrespective of the fact that he was inadvertently the architect of his own demise, this was nevertheless a young man who, like so many others, had travelled thousands of miles from a friendly nation (in his case Canada) to help us fight a war which wasn't his. That he was brave and that his heart was in the right place is in no way to be doubted.

(Further information on the Hurricane's wartime role in Scilly can be found in Rex Bowley's *Scilly At War* while Daphne Chudleigh covers the Isles of Scilly Steamship Company's war in her book *Bridge Over Lyonesse*).

98

Oh dear! The *Scillonian* ashore on Wingletang Ledge in 1951 after missing the entrance to St.Mary's Sound in thick fog.

The nearest the *Scillonian* came to firing a shot in anger was the regular test-firing of the Lewis gun that she had been equipped with at the start of the war, although the reason this had been fitted was made obvious during one trip when the *Scillonian's* crew witnessed an enemy plane attacking a coaster just off Land's End. As those on the bridge watched the German attack strike home, Captain Reseigh, mindful of the fact that it could so easily be their turn next, turned to his fellow crew members and bolstered their spirits with the words;

"We'll have a go if he comes for us, lads".

As Daphne Chudleigh records, the German pilot did not seek to engage the *Scillonian* and so the vessel's Lewis gun remained silent.

Fortunately, the war years passed mostly without incident, although for my grandfather there was the joy, in 1942, of the birth of his son Peter Joseph Reseigh who, like his father, would grow up to join Britain's Merchant Navy fleet. The young, professional sailor sailed the world's oceans until the mid -1960's when the siren cry of a certain young Cornish maiden ultimately

The real reason why Scilly has always needed (and probably always will need) a *Scillonian* – whether it be thousands of visitors, millions of daffodils or, as in this case, 180 tons of island-grown potatoes awaiting shipment to the mainland on June 1st 1948.

proved irresistible! Returning to port for the last time, Peter then made the successful transition to a shore-based career in banking. He and his wife Judith raised two sons, James and Jonathan. The elder son, James, followed his father into banking and even managed the Lloyd's branch in Scilly for a few years.

The elation shared by all at the end of World War Two, in 1945, was tainted for my grandfather by the loss that year of his daughter Muriel Hicks (nee Reseigh). Muriel suffered a painful and prolonged demise in St.Mary's Hospital from Hodgkin's Disease, which she she bore with as much grace, dignity and bravery as she could muster, but in the end it was a hard death. Step-daughter to Ena and half-sister to my mother Jeanne, Muriel was a kind and gentle soul who, God knows, deserved better than to go in such a way. While her brothers, Francis and Obed, were away at sea, busy in their respective naval careers, Muriel had become a close and cherished member of the family and her passing was a blow to them all but, as in every awful case where a child pre-deceases a parent, her father Joseph (and Muriel's sole remaining parent at that) suffered the loss the most.

Muriel's remains were buried in the parish cemetery on the outskirts of the village of Paul, high up above Newlyn on the Cornish mainland and not that much more than a stone's throw from her father's birthplace in Mousehole.

With the advent of peacetime in that year of 1945, life in Scilly slowly returned to normal. The *Scillonian* was repainted in her traditional white and she and her captain sailed on through the years and gradually grew older together. Along the way there was still the odd adventure or two such as occurred in 1951 when, approaching the islands in thick fog (remember the paucity of navigational aids?), Captain Reseigh found himself inching the *Scillonian* through the water seeking the entrance to St.Mary's Sound. Local practice in such weather was for the *Scillonian* to sound her horn on approaching the islands, while on land the then chairman of the Isles of Scilly Steamship Company, Rodney Ward (grandfather of Foredeck proprietor Terry Ward), would discharge a shotgun several times up on Normandy Downs as an aural reference point for the ship. Further along, on Peninnis Head, Vic Trenwith, island bus driver and a great local character, would assist by repeatedly blowing his ex-army bugle. Standing on the starboard wing of the bridge, my grandfather would wait until he heard all this off his right shoulder before judging exactly when to steer the *Scillonian* into the Sound.

On this occasion, surrounded by a blanket of fog which was, to use the island expression, 'thick as a bag', the *Scillonian* arrived off the back of St.Mary's in zero visibility and, at dead slow, began blindly working her way along the coast, which was just off to starboard. On deck the crew were watchful and alert, all eyes seeking that vital break in the thick, sprawling fog that would reveal, maybe just for an instant, the brief glimpse of a landmark to help overcome their disorientation and afford them some

clue as to the ship's exact position. Their ears strained unconsciously in the heavily-damped silence for those muffled, but welcome, blasts of the shotgun… there, the dull, distant cracks came and went, vanishing instantly into the murk. It wasn't much but it was something.

The *Scillonian* continued to cut forward through the glass-like sea, the trickling of the water from her bows sounding unnaturally loud in the eerie silence. Somewhere up ahead lay Peninnis Head and the next 'landmark' – the lone, trusty figure that would be Vic Trenwith, standing on the cliffs and ready to blow his old bugle in answer to the ship's stentorian horn.

The reassuring sound of the bugle never reached the ears of those aboard the *Scillonian*, the urgent notes swallowed up by the voracious fog. Up on the cliffs, Vic Trenwith listened intently as the *Scillonian's* horn faded gradually away to silence – the little white ship lost and invisible in the all-encompassing and all-too-visible white fog. There was nothing more he could do now…

Out to sea though, there was something Matt Lethbridge Snr. could do. Hove-to off Peninnis Head at the wheel of the Isles of Scilly Steamship Company launch *Kittern* in an attempt to rendezvous with the *Scillonian*, Matt set off gamely in pursuit of the vessel with the mournful sound of her horn his only uncertain guide to her possible direction.

On board the *RMS Scillonian*, time and distance seemed to alter. Having failed to hear the bugle, they'd lost that brief, tenuous 'handhold' with the islands and were now alone again. As the minutes ticked inexorably by, the realisation came to Captain Reseigh that he had sailed too far west, that they were off-course now, somewhere behind St.Agnes, and heading for the Western Rocks. My grandfather put the *Scillonian* gently about and, still in zero visibility, started slowly retracing his steps.

"Yikes! And awayyyyyyyyyyyyyyyyy!"

There was, perhaps, a degree of tension aboard the ship now as she struggled to find her way back and she hadn't travelled very far when there came a distant scraping down below which quickly intensified into a sinister shudder, as those aboard felt the deck below their feet suddenly start to rise. Passengers and crew reached out to brace themselves, thrown off-balance as the *Scillonian* was brought to an abrupt halt. She'd driven ashore on Wingletang Ledge.

Going astern produced no effect. She was aground hard and fast and so her engines were shut down. The *Scillonian's* horn now became a siren cry to guide would-be rescuers to her aid as the fog closed further in around the stricken ship. Aboard the vessel there was no panic, but a surprising calm as, under Captain Reseigh's supervision, the crew quietly and professionally mustered the passengers onto the steeply-canted deck. The ship wasn't taking in water and so, with no immediate danger present, there was nothing they could all do now but wait…

Back on St.Mary's, once the overdue *Scillonian's* position had been radioed in, the islanders went into action. The lifeboat *Cunard* was launched with Matt Lethbridge's son, the young Matt, at the helm. Venturing out into the dense fog, Matt eventually teamed up with his father in the *Kittern* and together, by instinct and dead reckoning, they converged on the *Scillonian*, still stuck fast on the rocks. After an orderly transfer of the ship's passenger payload, the two smaller vessels set off and managed to return safely to St.Mary's Harbour where the *Scillonian's* passengers, unfazed by their experience, were nonetheless grateful to re-acquaint themselves with the feel of dry land beneath their feet!

There were no casualties, of course, and the *Scillonian* was later refloated on the next tide with just a few buckled plates to show for the mishap. After minor repairs she went back into service just four days later.

There were lighter moments too, such as when Skipper, my grand-father's Jack Russell and a faithful sea-going companion, mistimed his return to the ship and arrived on St.Mary's Quay to find the *Scillonian's* stern pulling away from the quayhead. Without hesitation, the intrepid seadog launched himself off the quay into the water and proceeded to swim furiously after the departing vessel. Realising that the idiot would swim after the ship until he drowned, Captain Reseigh gave orders to heave to until the struggling, bedraggled mutt (but crew member nevertheless!) could be hoisted aboard.

However, the above were merely asides to the main story which was the transporting for over a quarter of a century (and, together with Chief Engineer Alfred Nicholls, clocking up a quarter of a million sea miles in well over 6,000 crossings), of tens of thousands of visitors to the Isles of Scilly, simply millions of island-grown daffodils and countless tons of cargo and other island produce – all of which forms the lifeblood of the economy of the Isles of Scilly and all of it useless without the means to 'bridge the gap over Lyonesse'.

In 1953, at the age of sixty-eight and with his health deteriorating, Captain Reseigh boarded the *Scillonian* as a passenger (a rare occasion, that!) for a journey up to London to The Royal Masonic Hospital, accompanied by my grandmother. He never returned.

His passing away came as a complete shock to the people of Scilly. As far as most of them knew at the time, their captain had simply gone 'up country', perhaps for a quick holiday such as he and Ena used to take once a year while the *Scillonian* was laid up in dry-dock for her annual refit. The tributes that began to pour in, once word got around, showed the esteem in which this quiet, unassuming man was held. It was the warmth of the tributes that was so striking, not just from islanders and locals, both in Scilly and across the water in Penzance and Mousehole, but from people all over the country, some of whom

Committed to the deep – the memorial service aboard the *Scillonian* following which the ashes of Captain Joseph Reseigh were scattered over the waters mid-way between Penzance and Scilly.

Floral tributes waiting to be cast overboard.

stated in their letters of condolence that they had only visited the islands a couple of times, but they remembered the kindly captain who greeted them so warmly on board the *Scillonian* during the crossings from Penzance to Scilly and back.

That was the secret, you see. People can admire skill and dedication, courage and commitment, devotion to duty etc, sometimes quite dispassionately but the vast majority of people respond to the human touch and Joseph Reseigh had that in spades. Once the ship was clear of port and his duties on the bridge temporarily concluded, he liked nothing better than to plot his chosen course around the decks of the *Scillonian*, pausing to chat a while with, quite literally, each and every one of his passengers. Some he'd met before, of course, so a chance to catch up with the news, others were first-time visitors so he'd enquire as to where they were from and then perhaps explain a little about the islands and answer any questions they might have. He'd also have a word of advice or sympathy for those passengers who looked like they weren't taking too kindly to the effects of the crossing (!), but to a man he was interested in them as people. Today, we have management phrases such as 'customer service' 'customer care' and 'pro-activity' but with Captain Reseigh it came from the heart, which, of course, is where it counts most.

Peter Reseigh, my uncle, once related the story to me of walking through Penzance with his father and being quite overwhelmed by the exchange of greetings that took place. A ten year old boy at the time, he later quantified the experience as being something akin, perhaps, to a stroll along the docks of Chatham in the presence of a 'Nelson' or a 'Collingwood'. Everyone, but everyone, knew 'the Captain'.

A few days later, with her Red Ensign flying at half-mast, the *RMS Scillonian's* engines died away to silence as the ship quietly hove to mid-way across the water between Penzance and the Isles of Scilly. A memorial service was held and the Captain's ashes, together with floral tributes, were scattered over the sea. The ship's engines chugged slowly back into life, a touch muted perhaps, and the *Scillonian* proceeded onwards towards Scilly... as she always does. So an era closes, so a new one dawns...

"Let not sorrow dim your eye,
Soon shall every tear be dry.
Let not fears your course impede,
Great your strength,
if great your need."

R.M.S. Scillonian, known and locked for almost affectionately by residents and visitors, was an unfailing link with Isles of Scilly throughout the dangerous navigation days of war. Tributes should be paid to Capt. J. Reseigh, the skipper, who is a native of Mousehole, and Mr. A. Nicholls, the chief engineer, of Newlyn, both of whom have been decorated during the war, and the crew for their devotion to duty in those days when the enemy might have attacked from the sea or the air.

HUMAN FOGHORN.—Mr. V. Trenwith, of St. Mary's, Isles of Scilly, has one of the world's strangest jobs. He stands on Pennines Point and blows a bugle to guide Scillonian into harbour during fog.

HIS BUGLE GOT LOST IN FOG

BUS driver Vic Trenwith blew his bugle through the Scilly Isles fog yesterday. But nobody heard him.

And the island steamer Scilloman (435 tons), with 70 people on board, ran aground on the Wingletang Rocks, off St. Mary's.

Many of the passengers had sailed from Penzance for a day trip to Scilly. The steamer ran into thick fog.

But with Captain Joseph Reseigh in command, no one worried. For the skipper has been

STOP PRESS

LONDON: MANCHESTER:
Temple Bar 1200   Central 3232

ARMS TALKS AGAIN

WASHINGTON, Monday. — Senior army officers from U.S., Britain, France and Canada renewed talks on standardisation of small arms ammunition among North Atlantic Treaty Organisation countries.—Reuter.

taking the Scilloman across this tough stretch of water for 20 years and won the MBE in 1942 for his services.

On foggy days Vic Trenwith stands on Penninis Head and trumpets a warning. But yesterday the fog was so bad that the steamer kept well clear of the point.

So Vic blew his signal in vain.

An island launch, the Kittern, which took some passengers off the Scilloman, went aground herself, but was pulled off by the lifeboat Cunard.

None of the passengers was hurt, and they all took the adventure as a joke. They hope to get back to Penzance this morning.

THE CHRISTMAS SHIP.

The good ship Scillonian
Goes rolling through the bay,
She bears a precious cargo
For tomorrow's Christmas Day,
And though a wild sou'-wester'
Is blowing half a gale,
The good ship Scillonian
Must take the Christmas mail.

The good ship Scillonian
Goes ploughing through the seas
With wind and tide against her,
But she little cares for these,
While in her hold, securely,
There are many treasures stored,
For this is the Christmas ship,
With Santa Claus aboard.

And there's Christmas fare a-plenty,
With jolly games and toys
For all the grown-up children,
Besides the girls and boys.
And Captain knows his vessel
And his crew will never fail,
For the good ship Scillonian
Must take the Christmas mail.

There are toy boats for Bryher boys,
(For doesn't Santa know
That Bryher men are boatmen,
And always will be so?)
And maybe there's a present
For those watchers of the night—
The ever-faithful keepers
Of the lonely Bishop Light.

There are dolls and drums and crackers,
And story-books of fairies,
For the children of St. Agnes,
St. Martin's, and St. Mary's.
And Tresco folk will revel
In the land of Make-believe,
When the good ship Scillonian
Comes home on Christmas Eve.

Ay, the good ship Scillonian
Is surely homeward bound,
Trim and white and stately,
She's steaming through the Sound,
For no matter what the weather,
Let it blow or rain or hail,
The good ship Scillonian
Will take the Christmas mail.

R. S. BEST, Boyton, Launceston.

SCILLONIAN'S CAPTAIN

"THE Cornishman" conveyed sad news to the Isles of Scilly when it recorded the passing in hospital in London of the beloved captain of the R.M.S. Scillonian. It is doubtful if in our generation any one figure from the Isles has been more widely known or deeply respected. A ferry ship is always more important than its master but for long the Scillonian will not seem quite so familiar without Captain Reseigh to either greet or comfort. It was probably a mortal blow when a cruel fog and relentless sea took his proud ship off course, after so many storms and hazards had been overcome with fortitude and skill. His complete wartime record was probably unequalled round our coasts, and his Royal honour gave immense satisfaction to Isles and mainland.

Boast not thyself of tomorrow; for thou knowest not what a day may bring forth.—Proverbs, **27,** 1.

Let not sorrow dim your eye,
Soon shall every tear be dry;
Let not fears your course impede,
Great your strength, if great your need.

DEATH OF CAPT. J. RESEIGH

MASTER OF R.M.S. SCILLONIAN

"The Cornishman" regrets to announce the death at a London hospital of Capt. Joseph Reseigh, M.B.E., J.P., of Auriga, St. Mary's, Isles of Scilly. Since 1931 he had been master of the R.M.S. Scillonian, and in that position had become known to thousands of people, both visitors, residents, and Servicemen.

Aged 68, Capt. Reseigh had established a reputation as a fine sailor and navigator. Throughout the war the boat, bound on urgent business at every voyage, never missed a sailing ,whether the odds against a successful crossing were bombs, mines, aircraft, rough seas or fog. In that time some 40,000 troops were carried and about 127,000 miles travelled, a service for which Capt. Reseigh was awarded the M.B.E. The same award also recognised the services of the Chief Engineer, Mr. Alfred Nicholls.

Capt. Reseigh was a Mousehole

Late Capt. J. Reseigh

man, and his brother and three sisters still live on the mainland, but he became "an Islander" and made his home there. His part in the life of the Islands was an important one, and was recognised by his selection as a Justice of the Peace for the Island Bench some eight years ago.

The Scillonian, wearing the Red Ensign at half-mast as she arrived at Penzance yesterday morning, was a little younger in the company's service than Capt. Reseigh, for he joined a year or two before the boat was built at Troon, Scotland, in 1925, but it was the Scillonian that made his life.

Her routine was his routine, and he took the same storms and buffetings in his life on board as came her way. Only the prospect of being unable to berth on arrival at St. Mary's kept him from taking his vessel across the stormy 40 miles of sea, for in the main the vessel has been the mainstay of the Island economy, and none knew better than her Master the part she plays in bringing in supplies and sending out exports to pay for them.

Capt. Reseigh married twice. There were two sons and a daughter who later died by his first wife, and a son and a daughter by the second marriage. He had been active until late in life, but in the past few months illness had troubled him and he had undergone treatment in London hospitals.

Shy of publicity and reticent to talk about himself, he nevertheless made a permanent place for himself in both the memories of those who sailed under his command and in the annals of Cornish seamanship.

The well-known and popular R.M.S. Scillonian, captained for many years by Capt. J. Reseigh.

Bows of the Isles of Scilly mail steamer Scillonian, damaged when she hit the back of the pier while attempting to enter Newlyn Harbour in heavy seas.

"Whoops!!"

The instantly recognisable wing shape of the Merlin-engined Spitfire.
Photo by Simon Jarman.

SCILLIES HAVE AN UNWELCOME VISITOR

ST. MARY'S MACHINE-GUNNED

ATTACK BY SINGLE RAIDER.

ST. MARY'S, Thursday.
Once again the tranquility of the Scilly Isles has been shattered by a visit from the enemy.

This morning a single German raider approached the Isles from an easterly direction and attacked St. Mary's with furious bursts of machine-gun fire.

Residents who were in the open at the time found themselves exposed to sudden death from the flying German bullets.

The attack was so sudden that the Scillonians were taken entirely by surprise, and the danger was upon them almost before they realised what was happening.

By what was scarcely short of a miracle, there were no casualties.

No bombs were dropped.

The raider, which appeared to be a Dornier, made off in a southerly direction, having accomplished nothing whatever, apart from giving the residents a nasty shock.

ENEMY OVER SOUTH-WEST TOWN.

There was also machine-gun fire near a South-West town on Wednesday evening. Tracer bullets ripped the air as a single raider flew past.

No incidents are reported, and most of the people in the town were unaware of the attack.

A Hawker Hurricane of the type used to provide the RMS Scillonian with an escort during World War Two.
Photo by Simon Jarman.

The Hurricanes of 87 Squadron didn't have the luxury of a proper runway like this when they landed on St.Mary's!
Photo by Simon Jarman.

dozen or so pilots and airmen required. Underwater telephone lines were already in existence, and one of them could easily be transformed into a scrambled hot line. Aircraft which went unserviceable operationally, but were in flying condition, could be flown back to Perranporth when relief aircraft would be flown out. Small ships could transport sufficient essential spares, such as VHF radios, sparking plugs, spare Merlins with a crane to install them, new tyres and so on. We would need camouflage netting for our Spitfires, because we would not want the Luftwaffe to appreciate that their all-important Milk Train was in dire danger.

The whole thing was obvious to me, and it was an essential operational requirement. I wrote a brief plan and showed it to Jack Boret, our Sector Commander. He read it and his wicked eyes pierced mine: "I will forward it with my strong endorsement" he said.

Nothing happened, of course. But if we had fixed the Milk Train, a great number of our major cities and ports would not necessarily have been blown up."

Why this plan never came to fruition is not explained. Like many ideas put

The *Queen of the Isles* – this plucky little ship was commissioned by the Isles of Scilly Steamship Company and launched in 1965 to run alongside the second *Scillonian*. After an economic downturn here she was sold in 1970 to the people of Tonga where she served their islands instead before moving on to New Zealand. In Tonga she ran onto a sandbank and spent some months there following a fire and, later on, was apparently wrecked during a typhoon in the Solomon Islands in the early 1990's… bless her little cotton socks!

The *RMV Scillonian* on her way to Scilly – taken from the helicopter. She took over from the first *Scillonian* in April 1956 and ran until she was herself replaced, in 1977, by *Scillonian III*.

The *Scillonian* forges ahead in rough seas off Peninnis on her way to Penzance.

forward at the time it quite possibly just disappeared into the corridors of power back at Fighter Command, never to see the light of day again. Maybe those back on dry land, charged with deploying Britain's meagre wartime resources, had to prioritise those resources elsewhere or, possibly, they were weren't quite able to see the potential of such plans as clearly as those, like Wing Commander Allen, who were out there in the front line. Maybe there were hidden logistical problems – perhaps mapping out a 700 yard runway was the stumbling block (Rex Bowley quotes the Hurricanes as coming in to land on 450 yards of St.Mary's grass with a hump in the middle of it!). However, if Wing Commander Allen had had his way, then those around at the time would have seen the exciting spectacle of Spitfires using Scilly as a springboard for the sort of Allied mission described above. If the damage inflicted by German bombers on English cities such as Plymouth and Coventry was the fruit of meteorological information supplied by the Milk Train, then it's a shame that Dizzy Allen wasn't granted the means to draw his sword and slash away at this particular German 'tentacle of war'.

"Byee! See you next year!" The *Scillonian* driving hard away from St.Mary's Quay laden with happy, suntanned holidaymakers.

Looking a little like a pair of gulls' backsides sitting on the water are the *Queen of the Isles* and the *Scillonian* moored together alongside the quay at St.Mary's in 1967.

April 1965 and a slightly watery sun shines down on the *Queen of the Isles* on the occasion of her maiden voyage to Scilly. Not many boats in the harbour of course and not many people on the quay, but look – a dog called Rufus is there to greet her.

A pristine white and brand spanking new *Scillonian III*, poised, in June 1977, to pick up the gauntlett thrown down by her predecessor. This is literally just before her naming ceremony – note the waiting bottle of champagne and the canvas obscuring her nameplate.

A few years later and, like her predecessors, *Scillonian III* is showing a few of the classic signs of wear and tear inflicted by the tough passage between Penzance and Scilly as she hauls away from St.Mary's Quay.

120

The scene over the Longships lighthouse (taken from the helicopter) shows the sort of seas typically encountered during the crossing to Scilly.

The Dutch cruise liner *Rotterdam* in 1963 and a regular visitor to Scilly in those days.

One of the largest ships ever to visit Scilly, the *Rotterdam* would slow down on her crossing from New York to Southampton and pass by to the east of the islands while a flotilla of island launches went out to greet her.

This is the *Nieuw Amsterdam (New Amsterdam)* off Scilly during the same period. She was a sister ship to the *Rotterdam* and there was a third vessel, called the *Nordam*, which also used to run in close to the islands. All were held in affection by the islanders – these were still (just) the days of the great transatlantic ocean liners.

March 1967 and the *Torrey Canyon* hard aground on the Seven Stones reef (wedged firmly astride Pollard Rock). These photographs were taken from the St.Mary's lifeboat *Guy and Clare Hunter* by the fondly-remembered and much-lamented Richard Lethbridge and reproduced here by kind permission of Richard's wife June. Thank you, June!

CHAPTER FOUR

THE WRECK OF THE TORREY CANYON

These days, with each and every shipping accident being automatically referred to as an 'ecological disaster', it is sometimes easy to forget just what a true environmental disaster can really entail in maritime terms. On Saturday 18th March 1967, when the *Torrey Canyon* steamed onto the Seven Stones' reef at a speed of seventeen knots (a legacy of sailing under automatic pilot deep into coastal waters) the modern world learned for the first time the full and frightening implications of the term 'oil pollution'. And this was no mere oil spillage. One of the first of the modern generation of so-called supertankers, the *Torrey Canyon* was a monster of a vessel laden with raw, crude oil – just under 120,000 tons of the hideous stuff, approximately half of which leaked and spewed out of her ruptured hull basting virtually the entire coastlines of Cornwall and Brittany in a choking, black, turgid tide. From north of Newquay all the way round to the Lizard Point and from Brignogan to Erquy near St.Malo, several hundred miles of the Cornish and Breton coasts fell victim to this evil, ecological assault. Lovely beaches both sides of the English Channel were simply plastered with oil, in some cases up to a foot deep, as in the case of beautiful Sennen Cove near the Land's End peninsula, one of the first, and worst, affected.

To put this disaster into some sort of perspective, consider the following: in 1989, another tanker, the *Exxon Valdez*, struck a rock and discharged some 30,000 tons of crude oil into an Alaskan basin, causing untold environmental damage and provoking a world-wide outcry. In 1967, the crew of the *Torrey Canyon* deliberately pumped nearly half that amount overboard in an attempt to lighten the ship enough to float her off the rocks. At that point in time, it seems, saving the ship took priority over the environment – an incomprehensible attitude by today's thinking.

The overall effects were catastrophic and Prime Minister Harold Wilson's Government struggled manfully to cope with the unprecedented consequences, as did his french counterpart across the Channel. Several thousand British soldiers were deployed to Cornwall to tackle the menace when it came ashore, while Royal Navy destroyers engaged it at sea spraying vast amounts of detergent (itself an environmental hazard) to break up the oil floating off-shore. The prime minister took a very personal interest in the disaster, visiting the scene and insisting on being kept fully up to speed with each and every development. As a statesman, Harold Wilson showed professional and equitable concern for Cornwall's plight, but he had a profound love for the Isles of Scilly and, privately, he was deeply worried about the potential consequences for the tiny, jewel-like islands.

The government, in a shrewd move, extracted some £3 million from the ship's owners by arresting a sister ship, the *Lake Palourde* on a technicality in Singapore – money which went straight into the 'disaster fund' as it were (a total of some £10 million was ultimately spent). The event virtually wrecked the Cornish tourist season that year as well as the Breton one. Typically, the greatest casualty was marine wildlife which saw tens of thousands of seabirds succumb, although heroic efforts were made by the local inhabitants to rescue and rehabilitate as many birds as possible. A dozen 'hospitals' were set up all over

Top left: An immense vessel in her day, the *Torrey Canyon* was laden with 120,000 tons of crude oil, nearly half of which escaped to devastate the coastlines of Cornwall and Brittany. Declared a total loss, she was bombed to destruction by the Royal Navy.

Left: Some of the crew of the *Guy and Clare Hunter* with the *Torrey Canyon* astern. Bowman Richard Lethbridge, along with his brother Matt (third generation coxswain) served aboard the islands' lifeboats *Cunard* and *Guy and Clare Hunter* for over thirty years.

Above: A Royal Navy Wessex helicopter hovers over the doomed vessel.

See the tiddly helicopter hovering above the stern of the *Torrey Canyon*. That's the Wessex from across the page and the Wessex is not a small helicopter! The *Torrey Canyon* measured 974 feet in length (57 feet shorter than the *Queen Elizabeth*), had a beam of 125 feet and drew 51 feet when fully laden.

The *Seven Stones* lightship towed into St.Mary's harbour by the Trinity House vessel *Stella* and moored for safety while the Royal Navy set about bombing the wreck of the *Torrey Canyon* in 1967.

Smoke rising from the wreck of the *Torrey Canyon* on the Seven Stones' reef in 1967, as the ship is bombed by Royal Navy Buccaneers from Lossiemouth – viewed from above Bar Point, St.Mary's.

The Sikorsky S-61N helicopter wheels in to land on her first ever scheduled flight to Scilly on May 2nd 1964 – the ground attendant's white gloves add a nice touch of class to the occasion!

BEA livery – remember that? In the foreground is airport duty officer Tony Thomas.

Cornwall, including the famous bird sanctuary at Mousehole, staffed by concerned volunteers who worked tirelessly to clean up and save oil-soaked birds. Shore-based marine life suffered and Brittany's precious oyster beds were swamped and took years to recover.

Coxswain Matt Lethbridge, his brother Richard and the rest of the crew of the St.Mary's lifeboat *Guy and Clare Hunter* set a then record for a lifeboat by remaining on station alongside the *Torrey Canyon* for thirty-two hours.

With some 50,000 tons of her cargo floating around the ocean, the *Torrey Canyon's* fate was finally sealed when Royal Navy Buccaneers were dispatched from the air station at Lossiemouth in Scotland to target the wreck with a substantial aerial bombardment. Hunters and Sea-Vixens from Yeovilton in Somerset were also brought in to assist and by the time the *Torrey Canyon* had been reduced to a smoking, blackened hulk ready to slip forever beneath the waves, some one hundred and sixty 1,000lb bombs, 11,000 gallons of kerosene, 3,000 gallons of napalm and sixteen rockets had been fired into the vessel. The resultant spectacle was like something out of a 'Thunderbirds' episode or the finale to a Bond film.

The *Torrey Canyon* was probably one of the steepest learning curves about oil-pollution ever inflicted on us and the lessons learned helped change our attitudes towards the environment forever. And Scilly? Despite being closest of all to the wreck, the Isles of Scilly miraculously escaped unscathed from the unholy contamination. Truly, they are the Fortunate Isles...

The full story of this momentous event can be found in *The Wreck of the Torrey Canyon* by Crispin Gill, Frank Booker and Tony Soper (Publisher David & Charles Ltd, Newton Abbott).

The paddle steamer *Bristol Queen* going astern from St.Mary's Quay in 1954.

...and ahead as she sets out to leave Scilly.

Above: The legendary Vic Trenwith resuming his role as bugler out at Peninnis for Westward Television producer John Bartlett (here on the right with his back to the camera) in 1972. Decades earlier Vic would use the bugle to guide the first *Scillonian* into the islands in thick fog. Scilly was a happy hunting ground for John Bartlett during the 60's and 70's and he produced several fine films about events in the islands' history. He regularly stayed at Auriga during his visits.

Left: Cloggy Mellor, The Hurdy-Gurdy man in 1960 – a regular visitor to Scilly. Looking slightly bemused is John Hicks, here aged five (and minus beard and gold earring!) who grew up to take over running the *Swordfish II* from his father Lloyd. Incidentally, the tradition of sailors wearing a gold earring in days gone by was a means, used by some, of carrying sufficient 'finance' to pay for a Christian burial should they die away from British shores.

"Thou painted Maypole!" The traditional dance around the Maypole in the Park in the mid-1960's.

1967 Carnival Queen Jane Hicks, daughter of Lloyd and Sue and a niece of Ena Reseigh, with assistants Myra Mumford and Linda Tresize either side of her.

Master boat-builder Tom Chudleigh puts the finishing touches to the gig *Serica* in 1967. Isn't she a beauty!

Mrs.Ethel Chudleigh performs the honours during the naming ceremony of the *Serica* on the Rechabite slip.

Lloyd Hicks – Dunkirk veteran and skipper of the *Swordfish I & II*.

Lloyd Hicks at the helm of *Swordfish II* ably assisted by Sid Lewis.

CHAPTER FIVE

BOATS, BOATMEN, BROTHERS AND BEARDS!

What became of those brothers that Ena and her sister Rene helped raise during their early childhood at Maypole in the 1920's?

Alfred John Hicks, known as 'Jack', born in 1903, was the eldest of the Hicks offspring but sadly didn't make it into adulthood. Plagued as a child with 'blackout' periods, he had an unfortunate fascination with guns (which were quite commonplace in those days, especially on farms) and although the family tried to keep the farm's shotgun out of reach, Jack somehow got hold of it one day and was later found dead in a nearby field, having had a tragic accident with it. He was fourteen years old.

Leonard Charles Hicks, the second eldest son and born in 1908, grew up in Scilly but joined Trinity House at the age of seventeen to become a lighthouse keeper. With no such thing as automation in those days, every lighthouse around the country, both on and off shore, was manned, usually by a 'crew' of two or three. Typically, keepers spent one month on duty followed by one month off. Leonard served on West Country lighthouses such as The Wolf Rock and the Longships off the Cornish coast and on the Bishop Rock off Scilly, but occasionally he found himself stationed further afield, such as on the Eddystone Light up near Plymouth. A month tour of duty is a long time, particularly if you happened to be stationed on one of the more exposed and remote lighthouses around Britain's coasts where keepers really were cut off from society. It was definitely a question of being comfortable with your own company as well as getting on with your fellow keepers, the more so during those times when bad weather precluded Trinity House vessels from relieving keepers at the end of

their stint. Such occasions were not uncommon. A delay of several days could ensue and, if you were really unlucky, you could find yourself marooned on your rock for several weeks. That month ashore must have seemed very welcome when it finally arrived!

There was one advantage, I suppose, to working for Trinity House in that lighthouses were, in times of war, considered key coastal defence 'installations' and so their keepers, as members of a reserved occupation, were usually spared the War Office call-up papers that most men received. Mind you the downside of that apparently cosy little perk is that, although the lights and beacons were dowsed during the war years, you would undoubtedly be a complete sitting duck should any enemy plane or warship in the vicinity decide to have a go!

ARTIST LIGHTHOUSE-KEEPER.
One of England's loneliest men,
Mr. L. C. Hicks, devotes his spare
time to painting. He is a keeper
of the Wolf Lighthouse.

A talented artist, Leonard occupied a lot of his spare time painting in oils and water colours and he achieved some very fine work over the years with canvasses depicting lighthouses, ships and coastal seascapes which are now treasured heirlooms in many of his relations' homes. There's usually a Hicks somewhere in each generation who holds the 'gifted brush' and today look no further than Stephen Hicks living on St.Mary's in Scilly, Leonard's great nephew and a fine artist in his own right. It's definitely a hereditary thing.

Upon retiring from Trinity House, Leonard designed and built himself a pleasure boat called the *Busy Bee* in which, from his base in Penzance, he took holidaymakers on trips up and down the Land's End peninsula. Married to Eugene they had two children, a son named John and a daughter named Connie. Talented in diverse ways, Leonard designed several other boats in his time but, sadly, he succumbed to cancer in 1950 at the awfully early age of forty-two – a cruel and unjust blow.

George Pezzack Hicks, known in the islands as 'Gee' (as in 'G' for George),

Gee Hicks brings the *Lily of Laguna* alongside the *THV Satellite*.

was born in 1910, a few years after his sisters Ena and Rene, and is rightly remembered as one of the more celebrated of Scilly's boatmen, skippering the *Lily of Laguna* from 1954 through until his retirement from boating in 1977. Pezzack was his mother Bertha's maiden name – she was originally from Mousehole.

As a young man, Gee worked alongside his father on Maypole Farm until, in his late 20's, he received the call to serve in the British Army during World War Two. Already in the Territorial Army, he was transferred to the Duke of Cornwall Light Infantry when the war proper got underway. From Northern Ireland at the start of the war Gee ended up in Belgium by 1945.

Following his demob. back into civilian life, Gee returned to Scilly and to Maypole Farm… and soon to a dilemma. With the imminent demise of his brother Leonard across the water in Penzance, Gee was to become the eldest of Alfred Hicks' surviving sons and, as such, would be next in line to inherit his father's farm as and when the time came, which it eventually did at the end of 1949. However, in times of war, a farmer's youngest son was traditionally spared the

military call-up and thus Billie, Gee's youngest brother, had remained at Maypole throughout World War Two and had been working to keep the farm going. Billie was only fifteen years old when he took the farm on in 1939 and put all the enthusiasm of his youth into the task, single-handedly accomplishing a great deal over the next six years. He realised, of course, that he was only temporarily in charge of Maypole and was fully expecting his brother to claim his rightful inheritance in due course. However, when the time came and Billie brought the subject up, Gee paused and cast his eye around the place. Mindful of the effort his fourteen-year younger brother had obviously been putting in, Gee simply drawled,

"That's alright, boy, you keep the farm – I'll find something else to do."

This was a gesture typical of the man's relaxed and laid-back approach to life but it underlined another quality common to all the Hicks' family – their innate ability to turn their hand to virtually anything and make a go of it, as Gee went on to prove.

Relaxed, quiet and placid, Gee was, as

Farewell visit to Scilly, in 1955, by the THV (Trinity House Vessel) *Satellite* (she was replaced by the *Patricia*). Islanders were invited aboard, hence the *Lily of Laguna* and the *Kittern* alongside. The *Kittern* later came to a sad end when she sank outside Penzance Harbour in the 1960's.

the above obviously indicates, a thoughtful man and this trait manifested itself in smaller, subtle ways as well. In an island community which never boasted a chess club, for example, he was a skilled exponent who indulged in correspondence or 'postal' chess with players who were sometimes on the other side of the world and it wasn't unusual for there to be several of these chess 'marathons' running concurrently. With each move worked out and then mailed to one's opponent, such chess games would literally take months, so you can also add 'patient' to my great uncle's many qualities.

Gentle he may have been but Gee was no 'softie'. Consider what happened when he accidentally hit his thumb with a heavy hammer one day in his workshop. The thumb started to bleed under the unbroken nail and by nightfall the pressure had built up to the point where Gee couldn't get to sleep. Finally, at two in the morning and fed up with this, he went down again to his workshop, put one of the finer drill bits into his Black & Decker and carefully drilled a couple of small holes in his thumbnail (eek!). He then squeezed the blood out to relieve the pressure and went back to bed!

In 1949, Gee, together with his brother Lloyd, commissioned the building of the *Swordfish* at a boatyard in Looe on the Cornish mainland with which they began fishing in the island waters. Round about the same time the two brothers also secured the Trinity House contract to carry out the Bishop Rock lighthouse relief, which they did for many years. This involved transporting keepers to and from the lighthouse by sea and using breeches buoy to effect the transfer between lighthouse and launch. Mail and other supplies were also shipped this way and it was always a major attraction for Scilly's holidaymakers to go along and watch this skilful operation. A veritable flotilla of island launches would accompany Gee and Lloyd on these occasions which, depending on the sea conditions at the time, could often prove an

exciting spectacle as waves threatened to pitch the relief boat onto the rocks while it manoeuvred around the base of the Bishop. It wasn't unknown for the dangling lighthouse keeper to receive a ducking in the sea as a wave lifted the boat and drove her in before the rope slack could be quickly taken up! Today, all lighthouses are fully automatic so there's no longer any need for keeper relief. Any maintenance required is effected via helicopters which land on specially-constructed platforms on the lighthouses, but it 'sure ain't so much fun'!!

Gee loved being on the water and it was very much a natural habitat to him. Never flustered, he always inspired great confidence in his passengers as he threaded the *Lily* around the islands' rocks and reefs, ably assisted by the likes of John Nicholls, Willie Williams, Keith Campion and George Mudge who all crewed for him at various times over the years and who all, doubtless, have their own stories to tell of their time with him (it'll only cost you a drink!). After landing his passengers on their chosen off-island, Gee would very often take the *Lily* off somewhere nearby, moor up and just take it easy, enjoying the peace and quiet. He once jokingly referred to his philosophy in life as being of the "Sometimes I just sits and thinks and sometimes I just sits" kind, but that would be to sell the man short. As a kid, I often used to sit and watch him tinker with the engine or else run deftly through his impressive array of card tricks and sleight of hand. An excellent wing-shot, I'm told that in the earlier days, before it became

Gee Hicks aboard the *Lily of Laguna* in 1959. Few people could coax a smile this wide out of Gee for a mere photograph but his elder sister Ena was one of them!

"After p***ing about for years getting picked off one by one, the shags and cormorants of Scilly finally got their act together..."

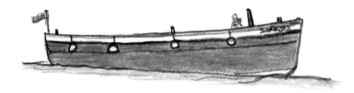

deemed environmentally unfriendly, Gee would occasionally take out his rifle and, having fired a warning shot to get the birds airborne (and to give them a sporting chance!), would pick off one or two shags and cormorants as they flew across the water. If this sounds brutal in today's sanitised world it must be remembered that, over half a century ago now, most seabirds were considered a threat to the small local fishing industry which was already on the wane. Shags and cormorants in particular consume a vast amount of fish and 'culling' them was considered as natural to island folk as a farmer protecting his crops and livestock against rabbits and foxes.

One of my favourite memories of Uncle Gee came about one summer when I'd spent the whole day with him aboard the *Lily of Laguna*, along with his dog Bilko (named after the 50's american TV character). We'd made several trips ferrying holidaymakers to and from the off-islands in gloriously warm and sunny Scillonian weather. Having dropped the last of the returning visitors off at the quay back on St.Mary's at the end of the afternoon, I stayed on board as Gee took the boat out to his mooring in the St.Mary's Pool. As we drew near I saw my great uncle's mouth tighten as he realised that a French yacht had tied itself to his buoy. He hailed the yacht's crew who foolishly started to object to having to move their boat. A brief but furious row ensued during which, glory be, I actually heard, for the first time ever, an adult utter the F-word for real. This was ground-breaking stuff in the life of a twelve year old kid in those days but, then again, if there was one thing that used to rile Gee it was finding a 'Frenchie', as he used to call them, on his mooring. Thanks, Uncle Gee!

Married to Laurel, Gee's sons, Michael and Alfred, and grandsons, Stephen, Fraser and Alec, today carry on the Hicks' boating tradition running the *Sea King*, the *Seahorse*, the *Kingfisher* and the *Pettifox* as well as retaining the original *Swordfish* from all those years ago. Gee sadly passed away in 1980.

The *Lily of Laguna*, now painted pale green instead of her former strident red, carried on in the hands of Guthrie Pender for many more years until the advent of new regulations, in the wake of the Marchioness disaster, finally started to mitigate against her. Eventually, one day she just didn't go back into the water, resting instead on her laurels up on the bank at Porthloo. The *Lily* struck a forlorn sight whenever I wandered round to see her, almost as if she couldn't quite understand what had happened to her – why nobody came along anymore to start her engines and steer her over to a boatload of waiting passengers, ready to embark on another trip to one of the islands. After all, that was her job, wasn't it, the job she'd been doing for over forty-five years now?

Salvation came in the form of a new owner, who worked away at weather-proofing her hull, while she sat proudly under a brand new awning bearing her name, until finally, in the summer of 2003, she put to sea again and was escorted out of the islands and onwards, bless her, to a new life in Falmouth. Maybe one day she'll make a return visit to Scilly…

Next to come along was **Lloyd Douglas Hicks**, born in 1917. Young Lloyd went straight into the Royal Navy at the age of sixteen where he served (for twelve years in total) in various parts of the world including a stint in Chinese waters during the Sino-Japanese war before the outbreak of the Second World War in 1939. His exploits during World War Two were many and varied and he was involved, along with

MORNING NEWS, TUESDAY, JUNE 4, 1940.

BIGGEST NAVAL OPERATIONS IN HISTORY

H.M.S. Basilisk, one of the few destroyers lost of the gigantic Armada of 222 British naval vessels and 665 other British craft which effected the withdrawal of the Allied forces from Dunkirk.—"The Western Morning News" Photograph.

St.Mary's pleasure boats in the early 1960's – left to right *Golden Spray*, *Gondolier*, *Swordfish II* and *Britannia*. Lloyd Hicks (on the foredeck of the *Swordfish*) is about to cast off while the *Lily of Laguna* (just visible in the bottom right of the picture) waits to move in. Alongside the far steps at the end of the quay lie the *Southern Queen*, the *Sea King* and the *Guiding Star*.

A few minutes later – the *Swordfish* has departed and the *Lily* has taken her place, while the *Kingsley* takes her turn to stand by waiting for the next boat to depart. Note the wheel amidships on the *Golden Spray*. Alongside the *Spray* lies the *Gondolier* which later left Scilly and went to Ireland where, sadly, she sank after an iron girder was accidentally dropped through her hull by a dockside crane.

Converted from ex-naval liberty launch to St.Mary's pleasure boat by her new skipper Lloyd Hicks, the *Swordfish II* takes to the islands' waters for her inaugural season on Good Friday 1963.

Shot of the old quay at St.Mary's from beside The Mermaid. The two white pleasure boats pictured are the *Nemo*, skipper Peter Thompson, and the *Silver Cloud*, skipper John Nicholls.

1961 David Badcock helps a passenger (his mother Rene, actually) disembark from the punt used to land visitors where there's no quay or, as in the case of Bryher in the days before Anneka Rice, when the quay's out of the water! In the background are the *Sapphire* and the original *Kingsley*.

done with the minimum of fuss by a man keen to shy away from accolades.

A strong, generous and forthright character, Lloyd could occasionally be a touch irascible and rarely stood for any nonsense. In fact, in his younger days he could, if required, 'clear a bar' virtually any old night of the week! I only got on the wrong side of my great uncle once but it kind of stuck in my mind for a while afterwards! I was eleven years old at the time and, one summer's day, a whole group of the family were bound for one of the off-islands aboard *Swordfish II*, on one of her scheduled trips. I was sitting amidships with my cousin John, Lloyd's son, who later, of course, grew up to skipper his dad's boat himself. John was only thirteen at this point and, boys being boys, he somehow ended up daring me to throw his swimming costume over the side of the boat. Of course, I did just that and John then had to go and tell his father who put the *Swordfish* about and throttled back, much to the curiosity of the other passengers, while the swimming costume was retrieved from the water.

Had I been a little more street-wise at the time, I should have perhaps guessed what was coming. The beard on Uncle Lloyd's chin was jutting dangerously (a sure sign of bad weather ahead!) as he stomped past me with a boathook hefted above the heads of the other passengers.

Just a few short years later, we're now on the *Guiding Star* and they're making them walk the plank! (Is that a mini-skirt on the far right?!).

David Badcock and the *Britannia* in 1972 – painted green on her arrival in Scilly, she was the colour in this photograph for thirty-five years until son David William took over at the end of 2002 and painted her *Swordfish* blue during the winter of that year.

Having snagged the costume from the water with the boathook, Lloyd swung round and the lights briefly went out as the sopping-wet trunks were 'thwacked' around my head. I thought I heard the words,

"Think that's funny do you, boy?"

as Lloyd swept imperiously past on his way back up to the helm of the *Swordfish*.

I can't remember now if it hurt or not but, even if it did, it was nothing compared to the humiliation that followed as eighty-odd passengers burst into spontaneous and quite helpess laughter at this spectacle! I suppose if this were to happen today I could look forward to years of emotional scarring followed by some intensive counselling but, back then... hey, it was merely part and parcel of growing up as a kid – you just got on with it! Fortunately, another of my cousins, Lloyd's daughter Ann, was on hand to render a comforting hug but I seem to remember keeping out of Uncle Lloyd's way for a day or two afterwards!

Big-hearted though he was, Lloyd succumbed to a heart attack in 1980 at the age of sixty-three – a truly sad loss. He and his second wife Sue had four children – a son John, who continued to run the *Swordfish II* until 1998, and three daughters Jane, Ann and Carol.

And what of the *Swordfish II* herself? From 1980 until the late 1990's, Lloyd's son John ran her (latterly adding a cabin and after deck) until, just before the turn of the century, John himself departed Scilly for pastures new on the mainland, leaving the Swordfish behind on St.Mary's. She was eventually sold, but, before she could leave Scilly, she broke her back on a rock whilst moored alongside the St.Mary's Quay. Beyond salvage, she was dragged ashore to be cut up and burned – a sad end to a her career as a fondly-remembered St.Mary's passenger launch, but not quite the end of her story. Her bow section survived and languished behind a wall down near Porth Mellin beach until one day local Scillonian diver Mark Groves literally came from Nowhere to rescue it. Now, adjacent to Nowhere over at Old Town there sits a strange object – something akin, perhaps, to a green-painted Bishop's mitre. The bows of the *Swordfish*, which shielded countless holidaymakers from the Scillonian sea-spray as she ferried them amongst the islands for over thirty-five years, now serve as a shelter for passers-by from those brief showers that so often catch the hiker unawares as he meanders round the St.Mary's coastline.

Brother number five was **Joseph Trenear Hicks**, born in 1920. Another young Maypole farmhand who went to sea, Joe entered the Royal Navy at the age of seventeen and was serving out in Egypt when war broke out in 1939. Like his brother, Joe also found himself at Dunkirk in 1940, although his experience of the evacuation itself was less eventful than Lloyd's. It was on the way back to Dover that fate caught up with Uncle Joe. Serving aboard *HMS Grafton* at the time, his ship's mission had gone well both at Dunkirk and, earlier on, in patrolling the English Channel on the lookout for German U-boats (good thing Horatio and Cuthbert did such a sterling job at Trafalgar or else I'd be calling it the French Channel...). The story goes that, returning to port in convoy, *HMS Grafton* fell victim in the Channel to a phalanx of German E-boats, the equivalent of the British MTB's (Motor Torpedo Boats) and was torpedo'd before the rest of the convoy could engage and drive off the enemy. Joe survived this and, like the rest of the Hicks' brothers, returned unscathed to his island home at the end of the war in 1945.

Mike Hicks glides the *Sea King* along the harbour in 1972. With her rakish looks she was a stunning addition to the fleet of St.Mary's pleasure boats when she arrived in the islands in 1963. Although she's since lost the mast and the distinctive engine housing amidships, she remains a good-looking vessel today. With the arrival of newly-designed fibreglass boats in the islands, the *Sea King*, the *Guiding Star*, the *Britannia* and the *Golden Spray* are among the last of the traditional wooden-hulled pleasure boats still in service.

The *Buccaneer* waiting for the *Guiding Star* to leave the quay at Bryher in 1970. Owned by Cyril and Garfield Ellis, the *Buccaneer* ran independently of the St.Mary's Boatmen's Association at this point in time.

David and Bennie Badcock – young guns here, in 1961, they have both recently retired after 40-odd years apiece as St.Mary's boatmen.

Gee Hicks manoeuvres the *Lily of Laguna* gently around the base of the Bishop Rock lighthouse while mail is winched up to the lighthouse keepers. This visit benefited from a calm sea – it wasn't always like that! (Photo by F.A.Webb).

162

After marrying his wife Betty, Joe entered the Coastguard Service in 1951 where he served thirty years based up at Telegraph on St.Mary's, keeping watch over many events which took place in and around Scillonian waters during this period. One such event was the *Torrey Canyon* disaster of 1967, whose 120,000 ton cargo of crude oil posed an awesome threat to the islands' fragile infrastructure. As lookout, monitoring the seas from the Telegraph Coastguard Tower for any signs of the incoming black tide, I bet Uncle Joe had a grandstand view of the oil-tanker, stuck fast on the Seven Stones' reef, as she was bombed by Royal Navy Buccaneers from Lossiemouth!

Gaining the Imperial Service Medal upon his retirement in 1981, Joe enjoyed the chance to spend more time fishing and lobster potting in his boat *Penguin*. Another one to enjoy the peace and quiet out on the water, Joe loved fishing and many times over the years he would pop into Auriga with a few freshly-caught mackerel or a "nice bit o' crab". Joe was, like his brother Gee, a quiet and placid man with a dry sense of humour, although this was severely tested one day in 1993 when his nephew John Hicks (yes, my cousin again!), while trying to reverse his old Mercedes estate car round the corner from old quay to new quay at St.Mary's, engaged the wrong gear, shot forward and dropped the whole shebang off the quay and onto his uncle's boat which was moored up alongside! Fortunately, there was no one aboard when this happened. It made quite a story in the islands at the time and poor Uncle Joe had to endure endless teasing about car-boats and the advantages of upgrading the *Penguin* to Mercedes power and so on. He took it all in good stead though.

Joe and Betty had two sons, Allan and Paul, and a daughter named Catherine. Joe outlived all his brothers and sisters and was the only one of his generation to make it into his 80's. A few short months before he passed away in January 2003 at the age of eighty-two, I remember thinking, as Uncle Joe chatted away on the phone to me about life in

the old days in Scilly and on Maypole Farm in particular, that these were moments to be treasured. It was a real pleasure listening to his rich, laid-back Scillonian drawl as he related stories from that era and it was particularly sad to lose that last direct link with a generation of such vibrant and colourful characters.

Last, but not least, was **Billie Pezzack Hicks**, born in 1924 and another son to bear his mother's maiden name.

As already stated, Billie, as the youngest son, was spared the call-up for service in World War Two and spent the war years working the farm at Maypole and giving over most of the flower growing to cultivating potatoes to assist with the war effort, as farms all over the country were doing. His father, Alfred, was quite advanced in years by then so young Billie pretty much had to do all the work himself but, with youth on his side, threw himself into the challenge. Thanks to the generosity of his elder brother Gee, Billie was able to hang on to the family farm at the end of the war which he then ran for the rest of his life. As a young man Billie was very much a pillar of the local community in Scilly. A church warden for many years, he voluntarily re-roofed the church hall when it fell into disrepair and funds for a new one were not available.

I once worked for my great uncle at Maypole Farm during a run of summers in the mid-1970's, when 'rival' farmers included such redoubtables as Barneslie Ward, Donald May and Melvin Bennett. A teenage kid at the time, it made a refreshing change from the rigours of school which was

The St.Mary's Sailing Club putting to sea from Porth Mellin in a variety of Tideway, Wayfarer and Mirror sailing dinghies. Lloyd Hicks built several of these sailing vessels for the club.

164

Stormy weather out in the Roads, viewed from Porthloo where the St.Mary's pleasure boats are laid up during the winter months.

Maypole flower farmer Billie Hicks (right) with stalwart drinking pal Dick Henry.

1972 and is this the author hard at work picking daffodils? Er, no… just posing actually! Some hard work on the flower farm did come along a couple of years later – although Dave Pearce, Maypole foreman at the time, might dispute that!

pretty much all I'd known of the world till then – in fact, it was an education in itself! Summertime is bulb time on flower farms and an integral part of the annual cycle. The bulbs need to be 'lifted' from the fields every so many years and taken back to the farm where they're then immersed in sterilising tanks to kill off the two parasites prevalent in this industry – the eel worm and the bulb fly. The eel worm lies in the ground and burrows its way into the bulb while the bulb fly lays its eggs in the neck of the bulb, the resultant larvae feeding off the tissue of the bulb until it's ultimately destroyed in a sticky mess. Once the bulbs have been treated in the sterilising tanks they're dried out and then put through a noisy, thumping, dust-generating grading machine (God, I hated that part of the job!) which separates the smaller, younger bulbs from the larger, older ones. There are several different sizes but essentially the larger ones are then bagged up and exported (Scillonian bulbs are even sent to Holland), while the smaller ones are re-planted in the fields to form the progenitors of the next crop of daffodils – and so the cycle goes on.

Working with my great uncle and his farmhands was a wonderful way to spend my summer holidays. Out in the fresh air and the sun-drenched fields of Scilly, clambering on and off tractors, loading lorries with sacks of bulbs and delivering them to the quay ready for the *Scillonian's* departure, with time afterwards, if we were lucky, to wash the dust away with a pint or two in the Mermaid, is a lifestyle I can recommend to any youngster seeking a bit of a break from normal society! Working alongside people like Dave Pearce and Jim Roberts (great guys) was

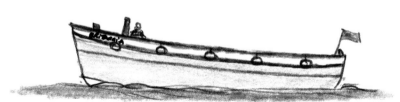

also educational and, as a less than street-wise college kid, I had to watch out for these 'salts of the earth' who considered me fair game for all manner of leg-pulling! They didn't catch me out too often although I did once find myself despatched to a neighbouring farm, after the tractor had broken down in the middle of a field, to procure 'a fornicating valve for a Ford 3000'. That, consequently, was probably the first four-syllable word I ever committed firmly to memory!

Billie occasionally used to join us out in the fields when we were lifting bulbs and brought his unique personality to bear on the day's events. I always enjoyed his company although you had to watch your back when he was driving the tractor down to the bottom of the field after we'd cleared each row of bulbs. My great uncle used to engage reverse gear and fairly storm backwards down the field, all the while scrutinising some ancient, tatty piece of paper on which he'd long ago scribbled 'which row in which field contained which bulbs etc.' and he never seemed to pay the slightest attention to where the tractor was going. Once, up near the St.Mary's Golf Course, he failed to spot that he'd reached the bottom of the field and the tractor just ploughed straight into the dry stone wall almost demolishing it. It was a good job it didn't because there was a drop of about eight to ten feet the other side of the wall to the next field and there was no safety cab on any of the Maypole tractors in those days. Uncle Billie just shrugged it off with a laugh.

He didn't laugh, though, when I stuffed his ancient Austin Cambridge estate car into the banks up at High Lanes in the summer of '76. We'd spent all day in the fields lifting bulbs when Billie spotted that market prices for new potatoes appeared to have peaked. Cornish new potatoes were a significant sideline then and my great uncle talked us into working four hours overtime that evening lifting these potatoes (by tractor headlight at the end no less!) so that we could run them down to the quay the next day and get them away to the mainland on board the *Scillonian* before that

Ena Reseigh with her sister Rene in Auriga — behind are their brothers (left to right) Billie Hicks, Joe Hicks, Lloyd Hicks and Gee Hicks with, in the foreground, Ena's son Peter Reseigh and his wife Judith.

A slightly larger group now, including Barbara and Betty Hicks on the left and Ben Badcock at the rear with Sue Hicks to his left. Laurel Hicks is in the foreground, while also in the shot are Bryan and 'Della' Bourdeaux, founders of the Bourdeaux gift shop situated in the narrow neck of Hugh Street.

The distinguished members of the Scillonian Club Committee, circa 1970. From left to right: Top Row – Tony Stock, Ben Badcock, Joe Hicks. Middle Row – Alfred May, Peter Nance, Michael Gray, Eric Guy, Albert Elvin and Jim Lethbridge. Bottom row – Steve Pearce, Sil Deason, Harold Wilson, Billy Watts and Bert Ball.

Ena Reseigh – after one of those swims!

The large family picnic on the beach — a feature of Scillonian life. All here are related to Ena and amongst them are two future St.Mary's Councillors, two future St.Mary's boatmen (the cool dude in the shades is *Guiding Star* skipper Joe Badcock!), a baby St.Mary's bank manager — oh, and a would-be author! Interesting what kids on a beach grow up to become, isn't it!

all-important market price started to drop. We finished the bulbs at five o'clock and I talked Billie into letting us take the car into town to get something to eat before going back to start on the potatoes at six.

Now cars in Scilly have never been subject to any formal MOT test and, while today general standards are monitored by the island police, back then you could drive virtually any old wreck and there were plenty around! Uncle Billie's Austin Cambridge had bald tyres with threads sticking out, a rusty colander for an exhaust pipe, marshmallow shock absorbers and about eleven inches of free play shared equally between steering-wheel and brake pedal. It shouldn't have been driven on the public highway at all and there was certainly no excuse for driving it fast – which is what I was doing as Dave Pearce, Jim Roberts and I raced back to Maypole at about one minute to six that evening. High Lanes is a twisty, single track lane near Maypole and as I went into the first set of bends (far too quickly!) the car started to drift further out than expected. It clipped the stone hedge on the outside of one of the bends, bounced off, hit the opposite hedge and then it was off with a mind of its own cannoning from hedge to hedge like some runaway bobsleigh on the Cresta Run while I tied myself in knots twirling the steering-wheel in vain.

Fortunately, the road was too narrow and the hedges too high to allow the car to get seriously out of shape and I eventually managed to bring it back under control just as we emerged at the other end. As the car rolled to a halt I noticed Dave Pearce, in the front passenger seat, sitting with both legs stretched out like ramrods in the footwell and both arms braced rigidly against the dashboard while in my right ear I became aware of heavy breathing and, turning to look, I found Jim Roberts' face (he'd been in the back seat) almost resting on my right shoulder. His eyes were tightly closed and his hands were up under his chin, the knuckles showing white as he gripped the redundant seatbelt hanging from the driver's door pillar to my right. He looked as though he was just about to ring in the New Year.

Unhurt, it was time to face the music. Uncle Billie frogmarched me around his battered car, triumphantly bellowing as he pointed out each fresh scratch that I'd inflicted (I honestly thought he was serious!) while completely ignoring the rust holes, pop-riveted repair patches and the absolute welter of older dents and scratches that had obviously been there since way before I'd even had a driving licence. Although I tried to atone for my misdemeanours by swapping over the doors from a similar but redundant car that Billie had in a barn nearby, I was subsequently introduced by my great uncle as his "car-breaking nephew" to any visitors to Maypole for the remainder of that summer!

These then were halcyon days for me, even if I didn't realise it at the time – happy, optimistic days, the period in life when you're young, when everything is possible and when you have the whole of the rest of your life ahead of you. So it was a shock when Uncle Billie died in 1978 at the age of fifty-four, the first of his generation to depart since Leonard in 1950. Billie and his first wife Barbara had two sons, Tommy and Eric, and indeed Tommy carried on the work at Maypole for many years until his own sad and untimely demise a few short years ago. Tommy's widow, Antoinette, bravely continues to run Maypole Farm to this day.

Finally, to round up the story of this generation (the surface has only been scratched, by the way!), let's not forget Ena's sister Rene (actually christened Irene) who shared the burden with my grandmother in those early days when cooking and cleaning, laundry and child-rearing was just part of the daily routine for these ten year old girls. Rene

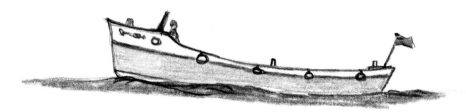

"Smile, you damn bird!" Lloyd Hicks snapping a puffin gamely held by wife Sue. This shot would join the hundreds of others that made up his famous slide-shows given in the Town Hall on a Sunday night.

The *Lily of Laguna* (poor old sausage!) up on the grass at Porthloo in the year 2000, after her forty-five odd years as a St.Mary's passenger launch had finally come to a close. Will the modern pleasure boats the *Kingfisher*, the *Meridian*, the *Sapphire,* and the *Osprey* (skippered by Alec Hicks, Jeremy Phillips, Joe Pender and Andy Howells respectively) invoke such fond memories in thirty-forty years' time? Yes, if they go the distance, I believe they will – nostalgia's a curious thing and only arrives when it's ready. (Photo by the author).

176

The Old Town churchyard – final resting-place of Harold Wilson, Ena Reseigh, Jeanne Reseigh, Lloyd Hicks, Gee and Laurel Hicks, Vic and Violet Trenwith, Richard Lethbridge, Bryan and Idella Bourdeaux, Bill and Joan Richards, Jim Roberts and dozens of cherished characters from the Scilly of yesteryear – fondly remembered. The Wall of Remembrance carries its legends too, with plaques dedicated to the likes of 'Fuzz' and Connie Groves, Jimmy Williams, Henry Thomas and Captain Joseph Reseigh – commemorated in spirit.

became a nurse and, aged twenty-one, left the islands to serve at the Battle Infirmiary in Swindon for several years before returning to Scilly to look after her mother Bertha who had started to ail before passing away in 1929. In 1931, Rene married Benjamin Badcock who'd arrived in the islands in 1926 as steward on *RMS Scillonian*. Ben later served in the Merchant Navy on tankers during World War Two and, following demobilisation, secured a post as Able Seaman aboard the Trinity House vessel *Satellite*, serving the lighthouses up and down the coast. He finally returned to the Isles of Scilly Steamship Co. as a stevedore working on the St.Mary's Quay until his retirement. He and Rene had two sons, Bennie and David, who have both very recently retired after clocking up over forty years' experience apiece as St.Mary's boatmen, starting in the early days in 1959 with the *Sapphire* before later skippering the *Guiding Star* and the *Britannia* respectively. As David has often been heard to say, "It sure beats working for a living!" Doubtless their own sons, Joseph and David William, who have taken over their respective fathers' boats would agree with that sentiment!

Sisters through thick and thin for seventy-five years, Rene and Ena only ever fell out once – once a week usually, whilst playing cards! Anyone who thinks domestic card-games are a light-hearted affair has obviously never been to Auriga on a Sunday evening in the days when Ena and Rene, together with their sisters-in-law Sue Hicks and Laurel Hicks, took to the baize! Good-natured though these games ultimately were, there were times when you could be forgiven for thinking otherwise! Bill Shankly, the legendary manager of Liverpool F.C. was once asked if Liverpudlians considered football 'a matter of life or death';

"No", he replied "it's far more important than that!"

With that philosophy he would have fitted right in during these card marathons at Auriga. Quite often there would be periods when the games were conducted in an eerie silence, accompanied only by the sound of breathing until suddenly someone would slap a card down onto the green baize table with a triumphant shout – accompanied by groans of disappointment from the others. Then the recriminations would follow;

"Well, you laid the card, you twit!"

"Well, you shouldn't have took it, you nit!"

Every so often, Ena would surreptitiously switch on the old tape recorder she kept hidden under a tea-trolley and leave it running to record these sisterly squabbles and it made for great mirth listening to the recording afterwards. Both Auntie Rene and Auntie Laurel were particularly fast talkers and in the heat of an argument would talk even faster – so fast, in fact, that to get all their words out they had to leave some of the words out – if you get my drift! Words like 'and', 'if' and 'but' etc. suddenly became somehow superfluous and were simply dispensed with such was their pace!

Born just over a year apart, Ena and Rene passed away within a year of each other at the end of their lives. Bless 'em both. In fact, God bless them all. They are together now, brothers and sisters all, in the picturesque little churchyard down at Old Town. When the gales blow and the sea roars into Old Town Bay, just the slightest breeze finds its way through the trees and into the sheltered little cemetery to disturb the peace of the residents within. But on fairweather days, when the sun shines down and the colours glow warmly, then those same residents can look out through the trees and over the tranquil, turquoise waters of the ever shimmering, ever glittering Scillonian sea.

"Fear not the dusk which closes in,
The tides of time that always win,
For young hearts soar and crest the waves,
While old hearts smile and gently fade.

They're watching now o'er you and I,
Since when did love eternal die!"

Jeremy Reseigh Watts on board *Scillonian III* in 1987

Ena Agnes Reseigh 'Grandmere extraordinaire'

ABOUT THE AUTHOR

Jeremy Reseigh Watts was born on St.Mary's in the Isles of Scilly in August 1957. Brought up in Virginia Water, Surrey and in Ascot, Berkshire he attended Windsor Grammar School for Boys from 1969–73 and Ranelagh School in Bracknell from 1973–75 before training, to become a French teacher, at St.Luke's College of Education in Exeter from 1975–78.

He then taught English from 1978–79 at the Lycee Pierre de Fermat in Toulouse in the south of France before returning to England and securing teaching posts in Dorset (teaching French this time), firstly at the Dorchester Modern School and then at the Convent of the Sacred Hearts in Weymouth.

Dismissed from the convent by the Mother Superior after one year (you can kiss a nun once, you can kiss a nun twice, but you mustn't get into the habit) Jeremy then took a summer job at Heathrow Airport in 1982 working for the British Airports Authority (now BAA Plc) which subsequently led to a career in aviation. After a number of airport operational roles he became, in 1990, a Terminal Duty Officer in Terminal 3, a position he currently occupies to this day. This job can be summed up loosely as 'roving troubleshooter and diplomat' on a good day, 'scapegoat' on a bad one!

Favourite authors include: Daphne du Maurier, Ian Fleming, Richard Hough and Thomas Hardy.

Interests include: the Isles of Scilly and Cornwall, photography, motor rallying, seventies' Italian sports cars, naval history, reading, writing and pseudo-intellectualising…

Jeremy Reseigh Watts
1st April 2004

WISDOM

"As the world ticks round the celestial clock
And Man seeks to define his role,
A question springs to mind:
Is wisdom achieved more through sorrow
than through joy,
Or is wisdom not the goal?"

'L'Oiseau d'Amour'
(The Bird of Love)

"She'll swoop down on her chosen prey,
She'll tarry awhile, she'll maybe stay.
She's sometimes hot, she's sometimes cold,
She won't be bought, she won't be sold,
And as for doing what she's told…!

She'll flesh your heart out, she'll make it swell,
You'll be off to Heaven… and maybe Hell!
But when she's gone, you'll miss her voice,
Just understand, it's not your choice…"

(for Carole)